Heroes of 1960s Motorcycle Sport

Off-Road Giants!

Other great books from Veloce –

Speedpro Series
4-cylinder Engine – How To Blueprint & Build A Short Block For High Performance (Hammill)
Alfa Romeo DOHC High-performance Manual (Kartalamakis)
Alfa Romeo V6 Engine High-performance Manual (Kartalamakis)
BMC 998cc A-series Engine – How To Power Tune (Hammill)
1275cc A-series High-performance Manual (Hammill)
Camshafts – How To Choose & Time Them For Maximum Power (Hammill)
Competition Car Datalogging Manual, The (Templeman)
Cylinder Heads – How To Build, Modify & Power Tune Updated & Revised Edition (Burgess & Gollan)
Distributor-type Ignition Systems – How To Build & Power Tune (Hammill)
Fast Road Car – How To Plan And Build Revised & Updated Colour New Edition (Stapleton)
Ford SOHC 'Pinto' & Sierra Cosworth DOHC Engines – How To Power Tune Updated & Enlarged Edition (Hammill)
Ford V8 – How To Power Tune Small Block Engines (Hammill)
Harley-Davidson Evolution Engines – How To Build & Power Tune (Hammill)
Holley Carburetors – How To Build & Power Tune Revised & Updated Edition (Hammill)
Jaguar XK Engines – How To Power Tune Revised & Updated Colour Edition (Hammill)
MG Midget & Austin-Healey Sprite – How To Power Tune Updated & Enlarged 3rd Edition (Stapleton)
MGB 4-cylinder Engine – How To Power Tune (Burgess)
MGB V8 Power – How To Give Your, Third Colour Edition (Williams)
MGB, MGC & MGB V8 – How To Improve (Williams)
Mini Engines – How To Power Tune On A Small Budget Colour Edition (Hammill)
Motorcycle-engined Racing Car – How To Build (Pashley)
Motorsport – Getting Started in (Collins)
Nitrous Oxide High-performance Manual, The (Langfield)
Rover V8 Engines – How To Power Tune (Hammill)
Sportscar/kitcar Suspension & Brakes – How To Build & Modify Revised 3rd Edition (Hammill)
SU Carburettor High-performance Manual (Hammill)
Suzuki 4x4 – How To Modify For Serious Off-road Action (Richardson)
Tiger Avon Sportscar – How To Build Your Own Updated & Revised 2nd Edition (Dudley)
TR2, 3 & TR4 – How To Improve (Williams)
TR5, 250 & TR6 – How To Improve (Williams)
TR7 & TR8 – How To Improve (Williams)
V8 Engine – How To Build A Short Block For High Performance (Hammill)
Volkswagen Beetle Suspension, Brakes & Chassis – How To Modify For High Performance (Hale)
Volkswagen Bus Suspension, Brakes & Chassis – How To Modify For High Performance (Hale)
Weber DCOE, & Dellorto DHLA Carburetors – How To Build & Power Tune 3rd Edition (Hammill)

Those Were The Days ... Series
Alpine Trials & Rallies 1910-1973 (Pfundner)
Austerity Motoring (Bobbitt)
Brighton National Speed Trials (Gardiner)
British Police Cars (Walker)
British Woodies (Peck)
Dune Buggy Phenomenon (Hale)
Dune Buggy Phenomenon Volume 2 (Hale)
Hot Rod & Stock Car Racing in Britain In The 1980s (Neil)
MG's Abingdon Factory (Moylan)
Motor Racing At Brands Hatch In The Seventies (Parker)
Motor Racing At Crystal Palace (Collins)
Motor Racing At Goodwood In The Sixties (Gardiner)
Motor Racing At Nassau In The 1950s & 1960s (O'Neil)
Motor Racing At Oulton Park In The 1960s (Mcfadyen)
Motor Racing At Oulton Park In The 1970s (Mcfadyen)
Three Wheelers (Bobbitt)

Enthusiast's Restoration Manual Series
Citroën 2CV, How To Restore (Porter)
Classic Car Bodywork, How To Restore (Thaddeus)
Classic Car Electrics (Thaddeus)
Classic Cars, How To Paint (Thaddeus)
Reliant Regal, How To Restore (Payne)
Triumph TR2/3/3A, How To Restore (Williams)
Triumph TR4/4A, How To Restore (Williams)
Triumph TR5/250 & 6, How To Restore (Williams)
Triumph TR7/8, How To Restore (Williams)
Volkswagen Beetle, How To Restore (Tyler)
VW Bay Window Bus (Paxton)
Yamaha FS1-E, How To Restore (Watts)

Essential Buyer's Guide Series
Alfa GT (Booker)
Alfa Romeo Spider Giulia (Booker & Talbott)
BMW GS (Henshaw)
BSA Bantam (Henshaw)
BSA Twins (Henshaw)
Citroën 2CV (Paxton)
Citroën ID & DS (Heilig)
Fiat 500 & 600 (Bobbitt)
Jaguar E-type 3.8 & 4.2-litre (Crespin)
Jaguar E-type V12 5.3-litre (Crespin)
Jaguar/Daimler XJ6, XJ12 & Sovereign (Crespin)
Jaguar XJ-S (Crespin)
MGB & MGB GT (Williams)
Mercedes-Benz 280SL-560DSL Roadsters (Bass)
Mercedes-Benz 'Pagoda' 230SL, 250SL & 280SL Roadsters & Coupés (Bass)
Morris Minor & 1000 (Newell)
Porsche 928 (Hemmings)
Rolls-Royce Silver Shadow & Bentley T-Series (Bobbitt)
Subaru Impreza (Hobbs)
Triumph Bonneville (Henshaw)
Triumph TR6 (Williams)
VW Beetle (Cservenka & Copping)
VW Bus (Cservenka & Copping)

Auto-Graphics Series
Fiat-based Abarths (Sparrow)
Jaguar MKI & II Saloons (Sparrow)
Lambretta Li Series Scooters (Sparrow)

Rally Giants Series
Audi Quattro (Robson)
Austin Healey 100-6 & 3000 (Robson)
Fiat 131 Abarth (Robson)
Ford Escort MkI (Robson)
Ford Escort RS Cosworth & World Rally Car (Robson)
Ford Escort RS1800 (Robson)
Lancia Stratos (Robson)
Peugeot 205 T16 (Robson)
Subaru Impreza (Robson)

General
1½-litre GP Racing 1961-1965 (Whitelock)
AC Two-litre Saloons & Buckland Sportscars (Archibald)
Alfa Romeo Giulia Coupé GT & GTA (Tipler)
Alfa Romeo Montreal – The Essential Companion (Taylor)
Alfa Tipo 33 (McDonough & Collins)
Alpine & Renault – The Development Of The Revolutionary Turbo F1 Car 1968 to 1979 (Smith)
Anatomy Of The Works Minis (Moylan)
Armstrong-Siddeley (Smith)
Autodrome (Collins & Ireland)
Automotive A-Z, Lane's Dictionary Of Automotive Terms (Lane)
Automotive Mascots (Kay & Springate)
Bahamas Speed Weeks, The (O'Neil)
Bentley Continental, Corniche And Azure (Bennett)
Bentley MkVI, Rolls-Royce Silver Wraith, Dawn & Cloud/Bentley R & S-Series (Nutland)
BMC Competitions Department Secrets (Turner, Chambers Browning)
BMW 5-Series (Cranswick)
BMW Z-Cars (Taylor)
Britains Farm Model Balers & Combines 1967 to 2007 (Pullen)
British 250cc Racing Motorcycles (Pereira)
British Cars, The Complete Catalogue Of, 1895-1975 (Culshaw & Horrobin)
BRM – A Mechanic's Tale (Salmon)
BRM V16 (Ludvigsen)
BSA Bantam Bible, The (Henshaw)
Bugatti Type 40 (Price)
Bugatti 46/50 Updated Edition (Price & Arbey)
Bugatti T44 & T49 (Price & Arbey)
Bugatti 57 2nd Edition (Price)
Caravans, The Illustrated History 1919-1959 (Jenkinson)
Caravans, The Illustrated History From 1960 (Jenkinson)
Carrera Panamericana, La (Tipler)
Chrysler 300 – America's Most Powerful Car 2nd Edition (Ackerson)
Chrysler PT Cruiser (Ackerson)
Citroën DS (Bobbitt)
Cliff Allison – From The Fells To Ferrari (Gauld)
Cobra – The Real Thing! (Legate)
Cortina – Ford's Bestseller (Robson)
Coventry Climax Racing Engines (Hammill)
Daimler SP250 New Edition (Long)
Datsun Fairlady Roadster To 280ZX – The Z-Car Story (Long)
Dino – The V6 Ferrari (Long)
Dodge Charger – Enduring Thunder (Ackerson)
Dodge Dynamite! (Grist)
Donington (Boddy)
Draw & Paint Cars – How To (Gardiner)
Drive On The Wild Side, A – 20 Extreme Driving Adventures From Around The World (Weaver)
Ducati 750 Bible, The (Falloon)
Ducati 860, 900 And Mille Bible, The (Falloon)
Dune Buggy, Building A – The Essential Manual (Shakespeare)
Dune Buggy Files (Hale)
Dune Buggy Handbook (Hale)
Edward Turner: The Man Behind The Motorcycles (Clew)
Fiat & Abarth 124 Spider & Coupé (Tipler)
Fiat & Abarth 500 & 600 2nd Edition (Bobbitt)
Fiats, Great Small (Ward)
Fine Art Of The Motorcycle Engine, The (Peirce)
Ford F100/F150 Pick-up 1948-1996 (Ackerson)
Ford F150 Pick-up 1997-2005 (Ackerson)
Ford GT – Then, And Now (Streather)
Ford GT40 (Legate)
Ford In Miniature (Olson)
Ford Model Y (Roberts)
Ford Thunderbird From 1954, The Book Of The (Long)
Forza Minardi! (Vigar)
Funky Mopeds (Skelton)
Gentleman Jack (Gauld)
GM In Miniature (Olson)
GT – The World's Best GT Cars 1953-73 (Dawson)
Hillclimbing & Sprinting – The Essential Manual (Short & Wilkinson)
Honda NSX (Long)
Jaguar, The Rise Of (Price)
Jaguar XJ-S (Long)
Jeep CJ (Ackerson)
Jeep Wrangler (Ackerson)
Karmann-Ghia Coupé & Convertible (Bobbitt)
Lamborghini Miura Bible, The (Sackey)
Lambretta Bible, The (Davies)
Lancia 037 (Collins)
Lancia Delta HF Integrale (Blaettel & Wagner)
Land Rover, The Half-ton Military (Cook)
Laverda Twins & Triples Bible 1968-1986 (Falloon)
Lea-Francis Story, The (Price)
Lexus Story, The (Long)
little book of smart, the (Jackson)
Lola – The Illustrated History (1957-1977) (Starkey)
Lola – All The Sports Racing & Single-seater Racing Cars 1978-1997 (Starkey)
Lola T70 – The Racing History & Individual Chassis Record 4th Edition (Starkey)
Lotus 49 (Oliver)
Marketingmobiles, The Wonderful Wacky World Of (Hale)
Mazda MX-5/Miata 1.6 Enthusiast's Workshop Manual (Grainger & Shoemark)
Mazda MX-5/Miata 1.8 Enthusiast's Workshop Manual (Grainger & Shoemark)
Mazda MX-5 Miata: The Book Of The World's Favourite Sportscar (Long)
Mazda MX-5 Miata Roadster (Long)
MGA (Price Williams)
MGB & MGB GT– Expert Guide (Auto-doc Series) (Williams)
MGB Electrical Systems (Astley)
Micro Caravans (Jenkinson)
Micro Trucks (Mort)
Microcars At Large! (Quellin)
Mini Cooper – The Real Thing! (Tipler)
Mitsubishi Lancer Evo, The Road Car & WRC Story (Long)
Montlhéry, The Story Of The Paris Autodrome (Boddy)
Morgan Maverick (Lawrence)
Morris Minor, 60 Years On The Road (Newell)
Moto Guzzi Sport & Le Mans Bible (Falloon)
Motor Movies – The Posters! (Veysey)
Motor Racing – Reflections Of A Lost Era (Carter)
Motorcycle Apprentice (Cakebread)
Motorcycle Road & Racing Chassis Designs (Noakes)
Motorhomes, The Illustrated History (Jenkinson)
Motorsport In colour, 1950s (Wainwright)
Nissan 300ZX & 350Z – The Z-Car Story (Long)
Off-Road Giants! – Heroes of 1960s Motorcycle Sport (Westlake)
Pass The Theory And Practical Driving Tests (Gibson & Hoole)
Peking To Paris 2007 (Young)
Plastic Toy Cars Of The 1950s & 1960s (Ralston)
Pontiac Firebird (Cranswick)
Porsche Boxster (Long)
Porsche 964, 993 & 996 Data Plate Code Breaker (Streather)
Porsche 356 (2nd Edition) (Long)
Porsche 911 Carrera – The Last Of The Evolution (Corlett)
Porsche 911R, RS & RSR, 4th Edition (Starkey)
Porsche 911 – The Definitive History 1963-1971 (Long)
Porsche 911 – The Definitive History 1971-1977 (Long)
Porsche 911 – The Definitive History 1977-1987 (Long)
Porsche 911 – The Definitive History 1987-1997 (Long)
Porsche 911 – The Definitive History 1997-2004 (Long)
Porsche 911SC 'Super Carrera' – The Essential Companion (Streather)
Porsche 914 & 914-6: The Definitive History Of The Road & Competition Cars (Long)
Porsche 924 (Long)
Porsche 944 (Long)
Porsche 993 'King Of Porsche' – The Essential Companion (Streather)
Porsche 996 'Supreme Porsche' – The Essential Companion (Streather)
Porsche Racing Cars – 1953 To 1975 (Long)
Porsche Racing Cars – 1976 On (Long)
Porsche – The Rally Story (Meredith)
Porsche: Three Generations Of Genius (Meredith)
RAC Rally Action! (Gardiner)
Rallye Sport Fords: The Inside Story (Moreton)
Redman, Jim – 6 Times World Motorcycle Champion: The Autobiography (Redman)
Rolls-Royce Silver Shadow/Bentley T Series Corniche & Camargue Revised & Enlarged Edition (Bobbitt)
Rolls-Royce Silver Spirit, Silver Spur & Bentley Mulsanne 2nd Edition (Bobbitt)
RX-7 – Mazda's Rotary Engine Sportscar (Updated & Revised New Edition) (Long)
Scooters & Microcars, The A-Z Of Popular (Dan)
Scooter Lifestyle (Grainger)
Singer Story: Cars, Commercial Vehicles, Bicycles & Motorcycle (Atkinson)
SM – Citroën's Maserati-engined Supercar (Long & Claverol)
Subaru Impreza: The Road Car And WRC Story (Long)
Supercar, How To Build your own (Thompson)
Taxi! The Story Of The 'London' Taxicab (Bobbitt)
Tinplate Toy Cars Of The 1950s & 1960s (Ralston)
Toyota Celica & Supra, The Book Of Toyota's Sports Coupés (Long)
Toyota MR2 Coupés & Spyders (Long)
Triumph Motorcycles & The Meriden Factory (Hancox)
Triumph Speed Twin & Thunderbird Bible (Woolridge)
Triumph Tiger Cub Bible (Estall)
Triumph Trophy Bible (Woolridge)
Triumph TR6 (Kimberley)
Unraced (Collins)
Velocette Motorcycles – MSS To Thruxton Updated & Revised (Burris)
Virgil Exner – Visioneer: The Official Biography Of Virgil M Exner Designer Extraordinaire (Grist)
Volkswagen Bus Book, The (Bobbitt)
Volkswagen Bus Or Van To Camper, How To Convert (Porter)
Volkswagens Of The World (Glen)
VW Beetle Cabriolet (Bobbitt)
VW Beetle – The Car Of The 20th Century (Copping)
VW Bus – 40 Years Of Splitties, Bays & Wedges (Copping)
VW Bus Book, The (Bobbitt)
VW Golf: Five Generations Of Fun (Copping & Cservenka)
VW – The Air-cooled Era (Copping)
VW T5 Camper Conversion Manual (Porter)
VW Campers (Copping)
Works Minis, The Last (Purves & Brenchley)
Works Rally Mechanic (Moylan)

www.veloce.co.uk

First published in October 2008 by Veloce Publishing Limited, 33 Trinity Street, Dorchester DT1 1TT, England. Fax 01305 268864/e-mail info@veloce.co.uk/web www.veloce.co.uk or www.velocebooks.com.
ISBN: 978-1-84584-190-4/UPC: 636847041908
© Andrew Westlake and Veloce Publishing 2008. All rights reserved. With the exception of quoting brief passages for the purpose of review, no part of this publication may be recorded, reproduced or transmitted by any means, including photocopying, without the written permission of Veloce Publishing Ltd. Throughout this book logos, model names and designations, etc, have been used for the purposes of identification, illustration and decoration. Such names are the property of the trademark holder as this is not an official publication.
Readers with ideas for automotive books, or books on other transport or related hobby subjects, are invited to write to the editorial director of Veloce Publishing at the above address.
British Library Cataloguing in Publication Data - A catalogue record for this book is available from the British Library. Typesetting, design and page make-up all by Veloce Publishing Ltd on Apple Mac.
Printed in India by Replika Press.

Heroes of 1960s Motorcycle Sport

Off-Road Giants!

VELOCE PUBLISHING
THE PUBLISHER OF FINE AUTOMOTIVE BOOKS

Dedication

To my big brother, Rod, who in the summer of 1961 started it all, and to my wife, Jill, for her wonderful support and encouragement.

CONTENTS

BIBLIOGRAPHY	5
FOREWORD BY MIKE JACKSON	6
ACKNOWLEDGEMENTS	6
TRISS SHARP	8
BRYAN 'BADGER' GOSS	14
GORDON JACKSON	20
BUD EKINS – AN AMERICAN ICON	26
CHENEY HISTORY AND THE BUSINESS TODAY	32
CHRIS HORSFIELD	38
DAVE CURTIS	48
FLUFF BROWN – AJS & COTTON	54
BRYAN SHARP – THE STORY OF NUMBER 70	60
KEN KENDALL	66
JOHN 'BURLY' BURTON	72
JOHNNY GILES – MR ALL-ROUNDER	77
IVOR ENGLAND – SMOOTH OPERATOR	87
KEN HEANES – MR ISDT	93
MAX KING	100
MIKE JACKSON	106
WASP – A STING IN THE TAIL	117
INDEX	123

Mike Jackson in action on the Greeves challenge, 1966.

FOREWORD

BY MIKE JACKSON

There exist innumerable old comp men with a passion for reading about trials, scrambles, and the ISDT (international six day trial), in that exciting period dating from 1950 through to the mid-sixties. The late Ralph Venables, discerning as ever, referred to this period as "The Golden Era," and with justification, because Britain was in possession of a substantial motorcycle industry producing state of the art machinery, with ten or more factories providing 'works' support for the day's top competitors. Many riders competed in at least two branches of the sport, and when it came to preparing or modifying their machines, they were (usually) technically competent as well. The contemporary competition scene, needless to say, abounded with interesting characters.

Following cessation of Deryk Wylde's superb *Off Road Review* after just 100 issues, and the sad passing of Ralph's column in *Trials & MX News* – which was part of our weekly diet – us old comp men were facing a famine of favourite reading material. Then out of the blue, circa 2003, came Andy! It is pleasing to report that Morton's Publishing swiftly recognized his talent, as well as the need for such material, with a result that *The Classic Motor Cycle* began running Andy's articles about some of the winners and notable characters from yesteryear's comp scene. These articles are happily now reproduced in *Off-Road Giants!*

Andy, of course, arrived a little too late to catch those early post-war giants: Bill Nicholson, Harold Lines, Hugh Viney, John Draper, et al, but with a portfolio that includes Gordon Jackson, John Giles, Bud Ekins, and Dave Curtis, who is going to complain? I confess I cannot now recall in which sequence the original articles appeared – it matters not – but the initial concentration was on his local West Country talent.

He revealed what it was that made 'Badger' Goss tick, and in writing about Triss Sharp, we learned how this successful 2- and 4-stroke scrambler was equally as creative in the workshop. Moving east, Andy then tracked John Giles and Gordon Jackson – currently resident in Devon – followed by trips north to interview Chris Horsfield and John Burton.

Nor did he stop with out-and-out racers. There's a fascinating profile on Max King, rider and broadcaster – and author of the definitive book on trials technique – in which is repeated that wonderful story of Max in the West of England trial, footing like a centipede, at which point Ivan Pridham refers Max to page 34 of his own book! Sidecar enthusiasts are handsomely catered for, thanks to interviews with Bristol's Ken Kendall, and Wasp's energetic proprietor Robbie Rhind-Tutt. Another manufacturing name on the Westlake visiting list was Cheney, this one covering the skills of father Eric and son Simon. Moving barely two miles up the road, Andy rightly put Ken Heanes – winner of umpteen ISDT medals, and much more besides – under the microscope. It was also good to read the life and times of 'Fluff' Brown, a scrambler in the fifties, and for years one of the motocross world's most prolific spanner-men. Oh, and Ivor England, a man who arguably headed the Rickman Bros as often as anyone; he too is the subject of yet another fascinating feature.

I know you will enjoy reading this book as much as your foreword-er did, for it's a feast of all that was fine in a time we will cherish forever.

Mike Jackson

ACKNOWLEDGEMENTS

Many thanks to all of the former stars – not only for their help and enthusiasm in compiling these profiles, but also for leaving a young Somerset lad with some wonderful and enduring memories from those care-free days of his childhood. For providing so many images, huge thanks must also go to Gordon Francis, Mortons' archive and the riders' own personal collections.

Bryan Sharp leading at the start of the 250cc British GP, Higher Farm Wick, Glastonbury 1962.

Triss leads Ivor England at a sunny Giants Head, July 1962.

During the '50s and '60s the Sharp brothers were among Britain's leading off-road riders. On a mixture of lightweight and heavyweight machines Triss reached the top in scrambles and international six day events, and, on his rasping Triumph twin, became my boyhood hero.

CHAPTER 1
TRISS SHARP

A cold spring Sunday in March 1961 is not a day that will go down in the annals of world history, but for an eight year old from Somerset it would shape the rest of his life. It's the day I journeyed to Dorset's Bulbarrow Hill in the back of my big brother Rod's ex-GPO 3-speed Morris eight van, and one that is forever and indelibly engrained in my brain. The roar of engines, the aroma of the burnt Castrol R, the vibration from the thundering speeding wheels – plus the taste of the hot dogs from the Cherry's catering van – brewed together into an intoxicating cocktail called scrambling. The names of many of the riders were known to me from my weekly diet of motorcycling supplied courtesy of *The Motor Cycle*, but now here they were roaring by a matter of feet away. The dashing and tigerish Bryan 'Badger' Goss forever on the back wheel of his Greeves, the brothers Rickman on their gleaming white Metisse, our local man Graham Wiggins on a screaming DOT, and the man who impressed me most of all and became my boyhood hero, Triss Sharp, aboard his immaculate Triumph special.

Fast forward over four decades and the lad – who used to fly around the local field with number 71 emblazoned across his push-bike – is now a full-time motorcycle magazine journalist with fond and crystal clear memories of that effortless Sharp riding style and his beautiful rasping Triumph twin. It was therefore a great privilege to visit Triss and his wife, Pat, at their home overlooking Poole harbour, where we spent a nostalgic afternoon reliving some of those halcyon days when scrambling was king.

At any southern or Wessex centre meeting during that era you could usually guarantee a winner wearing a seventy-something across his machine, as there was a sextet of international class riders – one that usually read Bryan Sharp 70, Triss 71, Jerry Scott 72, Derek and Don Rickman 73 and 74, and Ivor England 75, referred to collectively by Jerry's father Len as "the roaring seventies." That Triss and Bryan should take to motorcycle sport was not a surprise, as in the 1920s their father, Triss Senior, was a top class leg-trailing speedway rider aboard a Douglas. Triss Senior was captain of both New Cross and Crystal Palace speedway teams, although as his son told me, his and Bryan's first machine was of a rather more modest nature.

"The war was over, I guess I must have been about 13 or 14 and dad decided it was time for me to have my first bike, so he made one powered by a lawn mower engine, which both Bryan and I rode around the garden."

A muddy scramble on the works 250cc Francis Barnett in the mid-50s.

"2-STROKE TUNING WAS STILL VERY MUCH A 'DARK ART,' BUT COMPARED TO THE OPPOSITION THE SHARPS' BIKES FAIRLY FLEW"

1958 ISDT in Czechoslovakia, Triss storms up a steep climb on the works Francis Barnett. (Photo Triss Sharp archive)

Off-Road Giants!

It wasn't long before Triss had fully explored the speed potential of the 'garden special,' but in the days prior to schoolboy events he had to wait until he was sixteen for his scrambles debut. The Easter Friday meeting at Matchems Park heralded not only the start of spring but also the beginning of the scrambles season, and it was here in April 1950 that Triss first came under starters orders aboard a 125cc James. Not that he set the world on fire with his race baptism, as he explained:

"To say that the James was slow was an understatement. It struggled to get up some of the steep climbs and by the time I'd completed my first lap Eric Cheney had lapped me. Eric was well known to me because when I left school I joined Homesteads as an apprentice mechanic and I was put to work under him. He was a rear stickler when it came to cleaning and preparation, and my first job every Monday morning was to wash and polish his scrambler after the weekend's sport. And it didn't end at a quick hose down either, as he had me cleaning every fin with newspaper!"

This obviously stood Triss in good stead, because in later years the hallmark of both his and Bryan's bikes were their immaculate preparation and amazing reliability. At every opportunity Triss was either racing or practising, sometimes with disastrous results, like when he decided to 'field test' a customers Zundapp across the local heath land and returned it to Homesteads in a very sorry state – an escapade he was lucky not to lose his job over!

He was starting to get on the pace in scrambles, and also notched up his first win in a trial, the Sunbeam 2-stroke cup which younger brother Bryan would keep in the family by winning the following year. 1952 was memorable, as by now Triss had progressed to an ex-Arthur Wheeler Triumph Tiger 70 complete with a McCandless rear swinging arm, which saw him make his debut on foreign soil.

"Arthur Lambert had arranged for Derek Rickman and me to ride at Montrieul, which was an old chalk pit situated in the suburbs of Paris. We loaded our bikes onto the boat train at Weymouth which took us to Paris, and we then rode the bikes from our hotel to the track, competed in the scramble and then back to the station for the return trip. There were thousands lining the circuit, which featured a huge 20 foot drop known as 'Le Grand decent'. I can't remember too much about the race other than I fell off, but Derek had a good ride and finished well up on the leader board."

Like most of his peers, work was interrupted for the obligatory two years' national service, although fortunately it didn't upset his motorcycling activities too much.

"I was stationed with a night fighter squadron based at Badgate and was given a roster which included weekends. This would have put the kybosh on racing but after I saw the CO I managed to get someone to change with me so scrambling continued virtually unhindered."

By now both brothers were on works Dots, and along with team-mates Terry Cheshire and Bill Baraugh were starting to show the potential of the little 2-strokes in scrambles with some memorable victories. Back home in 'civvy street' Triss returned to his job at Homesteads before taking up a new position with Bob Fosters and some more antics, this time with a customer's Messerschmitt.

"With a separate set of points which opened slightly before TDC the Schmitt's engine would run in reverse using all four gears, so theoretically it was possible to go as fast both forwards and back. A couple of us decided to put it to the test, but the steering, which was twitchy going forwards, was absolutely deadly in reverse and in no time at all we were on two wheels and in great danger of tipping over. We over-corrected and went up the road going from front wheel to front wheel until we eventually managed to bring the Schmitt to a stop!"

By now Triss' silky smooth riding style was attracting other factory attentions, and in 1955 he got his first works Francis Barnett. A standard Barnett would only turn out a fairly modest 8bhp, and 2-stroke tuning was still very much a 'dark art', but compared to the opposition the Sharps' bikes fairly flew. This was largely attributed to the skilled hands of their father, 'Pops', who was held in high esteem in racing circles for his meticulous preparation. He managed to extract an extra 25 per cent of power out of the little Franny B.

An early outing on the works Greeves at Westbury-sub-Mendip, October 1959.

Not only did the Barnett's bring Triss numerous scrambles wins, it also rewarded him with the first of his four ISDT gold medals when in 1958 it was centred on Garmisch in the Bavarian Alps. For the British, the event proved to be disastrous; they lost men from both vase teams on the first day and Trophy man Brian Martin with a dead ignition on his Gold Star on the second. Perhaps the writing was on the wall, because by way of comparison the Czech's entered twenty 2-stroke mounted riders and all finished on gold!

But 17 British gold medals were won, including by Triss and Bryan on their works Francis Barnett's and Brian Stonebridge on

Triss leads Vic Eastwood (52), Don Rickman (74) and Jeff Smith (33) at the national Wessex scramble, Glastonbury 1962.

"TRISS WAS PARTICULARLY FORMIDABLE IN THE MUD, AND THIS HAD MUCH TO DO WITH THE LOW-DOWN GRUNT HIS BIKE DEVELOPED ..."

Off-Road Giants!

the factory Greeves 6 LHK. Francis Barnett was delighted with the achievements of its riders, and in recognition presented the brothers with sets of gold cuff links for their endeavours.

For many, of course, Triss' name became synonymous with his superbly prepared Triumphs, an association which began in 1956 when both he and Bryan were signed up by Ivor Davies to ride the factory twins. Although they were works bikes, he was given free rein to carry out his own modifications and improvements, as he explained:

"The Triumph frame had a tendency to flex, so like many I changed it for one from a BSA. Over a period of time I carried out numerous modifications, and the definitive version featured an Ariel rear swinging arm, Norton forks and Manx twin leading shoe front brake, BSA gearbox, Triumph clutch complete with rubber cush drive, the seat from a Greeves, and it carried the oil in the frame. It was still a weighty beast and tipped the scales at around 330lb, which was quite a handful, especially as I was only about 9 stone. The standard brakes were pretty marginal so I fitted a Manx twin leading shoe – which I got from Ray Petty via Eric Cheney – and cost me a whopping £100! Under race conditions the Norton forks would soon bottom out, so we would use the thickest oil possible to maintain some form of damping – when cold it was like treacle!"

Following the arrival of Brian Stonebridge at Greeves in January 1957, the reputation of the bikes from Thundersley flourished, and a network of dealerships and area representatives was set up. In 1959, Pop Sharp was appointed as Greeves' southern area representative, and shortly afterwards works machines arrived for Triss and Bryan. This heralded the start of a successful six year association between the Sharps and Greeves in both scrambles and the ISDT, and included many memorable highlights ... although Triss has particularly fond memories of winning the 100 mile scramble at Pirbright in 1961.

"As you can imagine, the event was absolutely knackering and called for good support and back-up from the pit crew for refuelling and the like. As an incentive the organisers not only paid prize money for winning, they also awarded money for lap leadership, and I went away from the meeting with £72 in my pocket. Pat and I were saving up to get married at the time so it bought our first cooker."

Continued success on both the works Greeves and Triumphs, allied to his obvious mechanical skills, saw Triss courted by the embryonic Bultaco Company and his appearance in the first Spanish GP.

"Bultaco was keen to get involved with scrambling, and was looking for both some technical help and top riders for the first big international race in Spain. I believe it had initially contacted the ACU which put it in touch with several manufacturers, including Greeves, who agreed to offer assistance. A group of us, including Don Rickman, Mike Jackson, Ian Horsell, Dave Curtis and myself, were flown out to Spain a week or so before the event, where we tested the bikes. Don had already done quite a bit of development work, but it was early days for them and the power characteristics were all wrong, there was no torque and, although fast, they were more like a road-racer than a scrambler and the suspension was very poor. The race itself was held on an old golf course near the centre of Barcelona, and watched by a crowd of about forty thousand. Don came first on a 175cc Bultaco followed by Ian Horsell, Mike Jackson and myself, and the crowd went absolutely wild – scrambling had arrived in Spain."

Despite his works rider status there was no fancy race transporter for Triss, and the bikes were taken to meetings in the back of his pickups; firstly a Morris Minor, although later he progressed to a Vanguard, which was eventually replaced by a Jaguar and a trailer which faithfully carried him to meetings all across the UK and to the continent. He was in demand by continental race organisers, and during his career raced in France, Holland, Italy and Germany, where by the mid-sixties he could command £100 in start money.

The hallmark of any Sharp bike was its immaculate preparation, and in more than a decade of racing the Triumph Triss only had one mechanically-caused retirement when a magneto failed. Of course there were other retirements through crashes and injury, some of which were quite spectacular and ended up with a visit to the local hospital, as he explained:

"I had several falls but undoubtedly the worst two were in the Isle of Man when I fell and broke my shoulder, and an early one at Wells which resulted in a broken arm. The Wells track featured a very fast downhill with a cross course ridge. I was going like the clappers on a Goldie when I lost the front end and the resulting injury kept me out of action for the best part of a year."

At the end of 1959 Triumph withdrew its works support, but the Sharps retained their factory machines and continued to develop them. Triss was particularly formidable in the mud, and this had much to do with the low-down grunt his bike developed, which stemmed from a trip to California that Bryan made in the winter of 1960/61. Greeves was keen to develop the lucrative American market and invited Bryan to take part in a series of desert races, hare and hounds and motocross events that included the famous 'Big Bear' meeting. Bryan showed his class and won seven races in the short season, and while he was there encountered both Steve McQueen and Bud Ekins. Steve offered Bryan a part as a BMW-riding German soldier in the film *The Great Escape*, but, concerned that it might be in breach of his contact with Greeves, he had to turn it down. Steve and Bud were well known for their enthusiasm for Triumphs, and what Bryan did bring back were some special cams which, when fitted into Triss' scrambler, really made it fly.

Not only did Triss notch up numerous scrambles wins for Greeves, the bike also took him to three more ISDT golds – although these events were not without their incidents, disappointments or controversies.

For the event in Austria in 1960, not only did the riders have to overcome the usual hazards of streams, mountain passes and forest tracks, they also had a major problem of spectator traffic. Riding for the British Trophy team, Triss was in collision with a private motorcyclist. Although both were unhurt the local police decided that action should be taken and, pending prosecution, impounded Triss' passport. Some time after the trial had ended Triss was given his freedom and a suspended sentence for 'endangering human life.'

More gold came in '62, but this was sandwiched between two retirements. In 1961 his Greeves sheared the gearbox mainshaft on day two, and in 1963 in Czechoslovakia things quickly went from bad to worse when, on day one, his bike steadfastly refused to start. It wouldn't respond to the kickstarter, and after bumping it into life his trial lasted only 5 miles when it locked up solid. Whether the reason was the low-grade petrol or an undetected lack of oil is not known, but for Triss the trial was over and meant an early return home, along with Gordon Blakeway who had also retired.

Not only did 1964 see Hollywood in Europe – when Steve McQueen, Bud Ekins and the American team entered the first event to

Triss Sharp

be held in East Germany – it also saw both Sharps win gold. The final special test was once again the speed test, and for many the highlight. They witnessed Triss and Bryan dice neck and neck for the whole of the 30 minutes on their Challenger-engined bikes, which proudly brought Greeves the manufacturer's team prize.

The following year saw the International in the Isle of Man, but sadly no repeat of the glory from twelve months earlier. Triss takes up the story once again.

"The weather was absolutely atrocious, with the island being battered by the tail end of hurricane Betsy. It rained incessantly, and in places visibility was down to a matter of a few yards. After manhandling our bikes out of bogs and mud holes all of the riders were soaking wet and totally dispirited. It was absolutely knackering just trying to keep going, and by the end of the day it was all you could do to pick up a knife and fork. Compared to the back-up the Eastern Europeans were getting, like hot drinks and dry clothing, ours was extremely poor. Sometimes you would get to a check and there was nothing!"

There was a general feel of dissent towards the ACU for not looking after the British riders better, and at the end of the third day Triss, Bryan and Pete Stirland decided enough was enough and retired. The daily newspapers reported somewhat sensationally that three British riders had been 'sacked', but this was a total fabrication and conveniently disregarded the awful weather conditions or the inferior back-up that the teams received. It also glossed over the fact that from the original 299 starters only 82 stayed the course, and only 18 of these achieved gold!

For Triss, the controversy brought the curtain down on both the works Greeves and the ISDT, although his scrambling career carried on for another three successful years aboard a 650cc Triumph Wasp. At the end of 1968 he called it a day, and the Wasp was sold to Frank Underwood and then to Badger Goss, where it was later stolen from his shop.

At the age of 46 Triss started his own engineering company, Stable Precision, which now supplies parts to Railtrack and the medical and aircraft industries, although nowadays he takes a back seat and leaves it in the capable hands of his manageress. The same meticulous preparation which went into those rasping Triumphs and crackling Greeves now goes into perfecting his golf handicap, and perhaps not surprisingly, Triss is quite a useful player.

In his last ISDT, Triss splashes through a stream on the Greeves in the Isle of Man in 1965. (Photo Triss Sharp archive)

Badger flying on the Greeves at a very cold Bulbarrow Hill in March 1963.

During the golden era of TV scrambles, Bryan 'Badger' Goss was a household name, his all-aggression style making him a favourite of many.

CHAPTER 2
BRYAN 'BADGER' GOSS

With his head down in grim determination and the front wheel of his bike pawing the air, none could better personify the 1960s scrambles scene than the tigerish man from Yetminster: Bryan 'Badger' Goss. And it wasn't just the trackside spectators who were privy to his superlative riding skills, as for the armchair fans Saturday afternoon meant their weekly diet of motorcycling with the BBC Grandstand series – a trophy which the dashing Badger scooped in the winter of 1969/70 aboard a Husqvarna. With the exposure generated by TV Badger Goss became a household name, but by then he'd already been racing for the best part of fifteen years and thrilling the vast crowds with his all-action riding style, a style I first witnessed at an XHG Tigers club meeting at the Giants head circuit near Dorchester, on a hot summer's day in 1961. That Badger won the lightweight race on his Greeves was not a surprise, but such was his lead he stopped to talk to someone in the crowd before disappearing in a cloud of dust, and then just for good measure popped a wheelie which took him the length of the start and finish straight!

For scrambling they were undoubtedly halcyon days, and ones great to recall when I visited Bryan and his wife Jenny at their south Somerset home. Thanks to the work of his sister Audrey the whole of B W Goss' racing career has been archived into a dozen or so bulging scrapbooks, but before we delved into them I asked him how his racing career started and how he got his now famous nickname?

"From an early age I loved bikes, but before I got one of my own I kept 'badgering' my friends to have a go on theirs, so one day someone called me Badger and it's stuck ever since. My first bike was a 197cc Ambassador which I paid £40 for, and I rode in my first scramble just after my 16th birthday. I also tried my hand at grass-tracking but crashed heavily at a meeting near Exeter and badly broke my leg, which kept me out of action for a year, and I vowed from then on it would be only scrambles!"

Young Badger's all-action and forceful riding style was wowing not only the West Country fans. He was soon attracting factory interest, and in 1959 became a works rider for Cotton. In an effort to keep up with the main Greeves opposition, the Gloucester firm had been working in tandem with Cross Manufacturing (Bath), perfecting a special linerless aluminium cylinder fitted with a semi slipper-type light alloy piston. It gave the Cougar a claimed increase in both performance and endurance, the potential of which was well illustrated by the new boy at Ham Hill near Yeovil. Against a host of the southern centres' top

On the very fast Cotton/
Cross Cougar in March 1960
– 5 starts, 5 wins.

Badger leaps the works
Greeves downhill at Higher
Farm Wick in the national
Wessex scramble, April 1962.

Off-Road Giants!

riders the rampant Goss rode it to five race wins in an afternoon, but Cotton failed to capitalise on this success and Bryan was lured away to Thundersley and a works Greeves. With the front wheel of his MCS high in the air, this is the era of his career that many of us remember so vividly, and one that Badger himself recalled with a great deal of fondness.

"Greeves was a great little company to ride for and always full of the enthusiasm generated by its two principals, Bert Greeves and his cousin Derry Preston-Cobb, who despite his disabilities would turn up at scrambles all over the country in his specially-tuned Invacar. When

Lots of concentration needed at a very muddy West Wilts scramble on the 250cc Greeves in 1964.

you got to know him 'Cobby' had a dry sense of humour, but above all both he and Mr Greeves were very straight men who honoured their word. At the time I signed for them I was driving a cattle lorry for a living, and after the weekend's race would often take the bike back to Thundersley in the back of the truck. The return trip was often done in the dead of night, and in the pre-motorway days I invariably got lost in north London and had to resort to the stars for my navigation."

Through a blind date arranged by his mate Dick Comer, Badger met Jenny. It was on a trip back to Thundersley on the Tilbury ferry in 1963 that Badger popped the question. Not surprisingly the answer was yes, but little did Jenny realise at the time how she would spend her honeymoon; Badger takes up the story again:

"By now I was starting to compete fairly regularly on the continent and I was booked in to ride at an international event near Lyon, which just happened to coincide with our honeymoon. It was arranged that Jenny and I would spend the first night in Paris and then travel on to Lyon, where we would meet my mate Don Hitchcock who had taken the bikes ahead in his Commer walk-through van. The van was equipped with a couple of bunk beds, but it was pretty rough and ready and hardly the bridal suite. We met up ok, but despite driving around for ages couldn't find the hotel we'd booked into, and with every other one full we had to spend the night in the van, Jenny and I in the top bunk and Hitchcock down below in the bottom. The meeting itself was a great one for the British as I won the 250cc race and Don Rickman raced his Metisse to victory in the 500."

There were undoubtedly good pickings made from racing against the world's best, and Badger recalled a particularly memorable weekend in Belgium when not only did he beat Torsten Hallman, he also came home with nearly £1000 in prize money. However, not all of his appearances were covered in glory, and I reminded him of a spectacular crash I'd witnessed at Glastonbury in 1962. It was the first ever 250cc world championship event to be staged in Britain, and on his works Greeves Badger was keen to impress; perhaps a bit too keen, as he told me.

"The Tor circuit was a long one, I think it was about a mile and a half and featured a very steep decent back down to the start and finish line. There was a double lip ridge at the top which slowed you down, but I figured that if you went fast enough it was possible to jump the second. In practice I decided to try it, but unfortunately my rear wheel just clipped the top of the second ridge and my Greeves and I cartwheeled down the hill. The battered MCS was wheeled away and I was carried off on a stretcher by the St John ambulance brigade with a dislocated shoulder; race over before it started!"

Like most of his contemporaries there were no fancy race transporters, and for Badger a trusty Morris Minor pick-up carried him and the works Greeves the length and breadth of the country.

1963 saw the opening of Bryan Goss Motorcycles, and for its owner a step into the unknown and plenty of sleepless nights.

"Greeves was paying me pretty well, and along with the money I was getting through its sponsor, Shell, things were looking good, so I located a shop in Yeovil which cost me £30 13s 6d a month to rent. I was racing Greeves so it was natural I should sell them in the shop, and my first bikes were an Essex twin and an MCS scrambler. Not only did Derry Preston-Cobb let me have them on a sale or return basis, he also stood as my guarantor with £500 of his own money."

Badger's shop is today run by his son Jeff (who incidentally is named after ex-BSA world champion Jeff Smith), and during the last forty years it has gone from its back street origins to be acknowledged as one of the south west's biggest retailers of clothing and accessories.

By the mid-sixties the era of Greeves' supremacy was coming to an end, and along with his team-mate Dave Bickers (who went to CZ) Badger decided it was time to move on. After a few rides on an AJS Stormer left him unimpressed he bought an ex-factory Husqvarna, and

Badger with team manager Harold Taylor and Malcolm Davis at the 1964 Trophee Des Nations in Markelo, Holland.

"I ALSO TRIED MY HAND
AT GRASS-TRACKING BUT
CRASHED HEAVILY AT A
MEETING NEAR EXETER

Off-Road Giants!

it would be the Swedish marque which would carry him to some of his greatest triumphs. During the next four of five seasons this would include victory in the Trophee Des Nations, the 250cc Grandstand trophy, and the British 500cc championship. Impressive credentials, so I asked him what he remembers about that first ride on the Husky and that memorable day at Brands when he trounced 47 of the world's best riders.

"Compared to my Greeves it was incredibly light and responsive, and on my first ride at Tweseldown it just flew and I won convincingly. I was soon winning regularly which the factory got to hear about and it supplied me with a works specification cylinder and exhaust. My old mate and rival Triss Sharp had earned an enviable reputation for his machine preparation, and as he was coming towards the end of his racing career took on the task of fettling and tuning the Husky, which needless to say always looked immaculate. It was a great honour when I was asked by the ACU to represent the British team that included Dave Bickers, Fred Mayes and the Rickman brothers for the 1966 Trophee Des Nations. It wasn't so great, however, to hear at the pre-race team talk that the British manager regarded me as 'the weak link of the team'."

Whether this was a clever tactical ploy or not we shall probably never know, but to Badger the gauntlet was thrown down and he responded in the best possible way. The gate dropped and with a cacophony of noise and a huge cloud of smoke the field flew into the first bend, with the fired-up Badger holding fourth place. The vast crowd that day saw both the Goss riding skill and tenacity at its best, and as the race progressed not only did they see him grab the lead, he drew away to win by a staggering 34 seconds from second-placed Dave Bickers. A fantastic win, but in the process the Husqvarna had taken quite a hammering, as he explained.

"By the end of the first leg the Husky had received one hell of a bashing and the spokes in the rear wheel were virtually hanging out. My race mechanic, Jack Hooper, worked wonders between races rebuilding the wheel, so I lined up for the second leg feeling pretty confident."

Just to prove that race one was no fluke Badger shot away with the pack, and by three quarter distance was in the lead. From then on the racing was for the podium and team positions, and on the fall of the flag B W Goss was victor by an impressive 25 seconds over world champion Joel Robert, and the crowd went absolutely wild with delight. Despite Badgers efforts the British couldn't finish in depth, and the Swedes, led by Torsten Hallman, took the team trophy although they were less than gracious and insisted that Badger's motor be stripped down, as they were convinced he was riding a 360cc. Measurement proved otherwise and they had to begrudgingly concede that they had been beaten by the best man on the day.

Spurred on by success in the Trophee, the seasons of 1967-69 saw Badger and the works specification Husqvarna's on the world championship trail. By now his race transport was a 2-litre Capri and trailer in which travelled as far east as Russia in search of championship points. Despite some steady rides there was nothing outstanding to report, and a fourth was his best result, although in the team events he continued to excel. For the 1967 Trophee Des Nations the British had to travel to Holitz in Czechoslovakia, and the long journey was rewarded when Badger screamed the Husky to victory in race one. Hopes of a repeat of the previous year, however, were dashed when in race two a screw in the forks became detached; robbed of some much needed damping, he limped home in 12th position.

On the home front the name of Goss was permanently in the results, and victory in the ever popular 1969 250cc Grandstand trophy series was followed the next season when he scooped the 500cc British championship. Aboard the big Husky this was perhaps his finest hour, as he had to balance his will to win with season length consistency and he eventually ran out 16 points clear of his nearest challenger, Keith Hickman on the works BSA. Befitting a champion, he had now progressed to driving a top of the range 3-litre Capri, which along with a trailer was used to transport the bike and the Goss family of Bryan, Jenny and children Jeff and Debbie to meetings all over the UK and Europe.

Throughout his career Badger was never one to rest on his laurels, and always had an eye open for better machinery and business opportunities; both came his way in 1971.

"Maico was starting to get some good results in the world championships, and although I hadn't seen one in the UK I did some detective work and discovered it had an importer based in Bolton. I contacted him and asked for a bike to try out, but he was totally uninterested so perhaps it was no surprise that Maico's were little heard of here. Undeterred, I contacted the factory, and compared to the response I'd got from Bolton they were incredibly enthusiastic and the export manager Hans Kriesen invited me to the works. I drove to Stuttgart in my Mini Cooper and on arrival expected to see an ultra-modern production facility, but in fact the factory was old fashioned and the bikes had the appearance of being homemade and rather crude. This was deceptive because what they lacked in looks they more than made up for in performance and rugged durability, and just from my initial ride around the test track it was obvious that they had an extremely competitive bike. So with test completed a deal was done, and I drove back to England with a stripped down Maico in the back of the Mini."

Back home, the Goss-Maico combination made an impressive debut in a TV scramble at Dyram Park near Bristol, and soon others were eagerly trying to get their hands on one of the West German 2-strokes. Not only was Badger an extremely talented and tenacious rider, he also had an eye for business, and this was rewarded when he was appointed as Maico's UK importer. From his early days he was acutely aware of the old saying 'a win on Sunday, a sale on Monday' and he soon had an impressive setup of dealerships and supported riders under his wing, which included Gerald Windsor, Rob Taylor and Tom Leadbitter. Almost anyone who was anyone in the motocross field wanted to be seen on a Maico, and Badger had to work flat out supplying an ever burgeoning demand.

"It was no good having customers who wanted the bikes and then not being able to supply them with one, so right from our early days with Maico we made sure that we had plenty of stock and spares, so every fortnight we would send a truck to load up with 36 bikes – which, incidentally, was the factory's output for a day. They were not only fast, they were fantastically reliable, and for three years on the trot we sold over a thousand bikes a year, which for a small concern like us was like winning the pools!"

As the decade progressed much of his energies were channelled into the business, and after 20 years of top flight racing he retired in 1977. With the demise of Maico he later took over from Comerfords as KTM importer, and also became importer for White Power shocks

Bryan 'Badger' Goss

and Barum tyres. Always willing to give plenty back to the sport he loved, the list of people sponsored by Badger reads like a who's who of world class riders, and includes Neil Hudson, Graham Noyce, enduro champion Geraint Jones, and the Dark Lane team managed by his good mate Mick Dayler. Whether in racing or business, the same Goss drive, determination and enthusiasm have always been evident, but Bryan is quick to acknowledge all of the help he's received along the way, especially from Jenny, Jeff and Debbie and his closely knit family. Only once was he lured out of retirement, to a meeting at Bridport where he raced and won on a 650cc Triumph Wasp; incidentally, the bike had been previously owned by his old mate and rival Triss Sharp, and it was Badger's first and last race on a 4-stroke.

Badger is still full of enthusiasm for motorcycling, although he now seldom attends meetings and has his diet of racing supplied courtesy of the TV. In the sixties it was scrambling and the name of Goss which was brought into the nation's front rooms, but now it's the speed and thrills of the Moto GP which has the viewers glued to their sets – and interestingly, a man racing under the number 46 is one of the best in the world. Some things never change, do they?

An early outing on the 250cc Husqvarna at Bulbarrow Hill in October 1965.

> "WHETHER IN RACING OR BUSINESS, THE SAME GOSS DRIVE, DETERMINATION AND ENTHUSIASM HAVE ALWAYS BEEN EVIDENT"

Yet another clean [zero penalty points] in the Bath club's Kickham trial in 1961.

CHAPTER 3
GORDON JACKSON

Through much of the 1950s and early 1960s AMC-mounted Gordon Jackson was one of the top men in the feet-up game, winning the prestigious Scottish six days trial no fewer than four times, including the famous one dab victory in 1961.

It's the Tuesday of the 1961 Scottish six days trial, and at Grey Mares Ridge works AJS man Gordon Jackson is forced to dab; that same second the fateful foot is caught on camera by journalist Peter Howdle. In normal circumstances the sight of a trials rider losing a mark would be nothing unusual, but for the star AMC man it would prove to be his only loss of marks, and Howdle's photograph would become one of trials most famous images. Jackson's solitary dab was enough to give the then twenty-nine year old man of Kent a four mark winning margin over runner-up Sammy Miller, and his fourth victory in what is arguably one of trials' most famous and arduous events. Twelve months later the roles would be reversed, but by the end of '62 Gordon called it a day and at the age of thirty brought the curtain down on his hugely successful motorcycling career – one in which out of eleven starts he only once finished outside the top three in the Scottish, became twice overall winner of the British championship (once in its earlier guise of ACU solo trials star) and scooped the prestigious British Experts trial, plus numerous other trade supported nationals and many open to centre and club events. Just for good measure he also became a very accomplished scrambler, and to add to his impressive off-road CV he later – in 1980 – won the British trials car championship, the only man to achieve this on both two and four wheels. To find out more about this remarkably talented competitor I visited Gordon at his north Devon home where we spent several enjoyable hours reliving those golden days.

Brought up on a farm and with a father who liked motorcycles it's perhaps not surprising to learn that the young Jackson soon had a bike, although as he told me his choice didn't immediately meet with great parental approval.

"Although my dad didn't ride competitively he was a good friend of the Collier brothers, and in the early twenties he would often join them for Sunday rides to Box Hill and the like on his Matchless. I actually bought my first bike, a 1928 flat tank 500cc Norton, from two older lads for £3 10s when I was only nine years old; this was quite a sum of money, as I think my total savings at the time was about £4. The secret to getting it started was to pour a tin of lighter fuel into the carb, and once running turn on the tap to the tank which contained tractor vaporising oil (TVO); needless to say it smoked rather a lot! I hid it in one of our barns but my dad had a fit when he discovered it, the Norton was far too big for me, so after about three weeks we sold it and replaced it with a much more suitable 125cc Villiers-engined bike."

Gordon concentrating his way to another clean in the 1962 Scottish six days trial, in which he was runner-up.

Off-Road Giants!

Flying around the farm on the little 2-stroke certainly taught the young Gordon a lot about throttle control and balance, skills which he would use to great effect when he started trialling.

"I was still at school when racing restarted after the Second World War, and the first meeting I attended was a scramble at Brands Hatch in 1948. It was only about eight miles or so from our farm, so when someone told me that the following week the local club was organising a trial I decided to go back and see what it was all about. Up until then, of course, all of what I knew about scrambles and trials was what I'd read in the pages of The Motorcycle and Motorcycling. It was great, and as there seemed to be a lot more trials than scrambles I decided that I'd have a go at the feet up game. I'd been working on the farm during the holidays so from the money saved bought myself a 350cc Matchless; a bike which had started life as an army issue machine but had been built into comp spec by Joe Francis. Membership of my local Sidcup club was full, so I joined the Double Five and made my debut in one of its closed to club trials."

It was not only Gordon who was starting out that day, but another young man who would also become a top scramble, trials and international six days rider, Johnny Giles. It was the start of a friendship between the two which has endured to this day, so I asked Gordon about those early days before he became a works supported rider; days when the only way to get to and from an event was on the bike.

"During the next couple of years both Johnny and I gradually improved and began picking up the odd first and second class awards in open to centre trials. Our ambition was to become works riders, so we decided to spread our wings a bit to do some events further afield. At that time there was no possibility of being able to afford a car and trailer or pick-up, so the only way to get there and back was to fit bobby dodgers and ride the bikes. Gilo had got a 500T Norton on which he'd managed to win the Stretham trophy, so I thought that I'd better follow suite; it was a good bike and my first win came in the Rochester club's Williams trophy trial in October 1950."

Acutely aware that the AMC works was only twelve miles away, Jackson thought that a change to a Plumstead single might enhance his chances of a factory ride. Therefore, in 1951 he bought himself a 500cc Matchless, a bike which carried him not only to the 500cc cup in the southern Experts but also one he rode in far away Northumberland; a memorable trip which he told me about.

"Johnny and I had entered the Travers trial and arranged to meet Matchless teamster Ted Usher and Ray Peacock at the Dutch house in south London. Johnny had managed to borrow his father's car, so the idea was that we would all travel together in convoy with the journey broken by an overnight stop on the way. This was all in pre-motorway days, so it was a long old trip and one not helped when the radiator of Usher's car started to boil. Gilo and I managed to get some water from a farm and he limped on to Grantham where we bought and fitted a replacement. Things then went from bad to worse when his clutch started to slip. This resulted in Johnny and I having to get out and push it up a particularly steep hill, then on arrival at St Johns Chapel we discovered that the pub we'd booked into for the night had already shut. Ted and Ray were in another close by – which fortunately was still open – so there was no other option than for the four of us to share a 'family' room, Ted in the single bed with Ray, John and I head to toe in the double. Incidentally, BSA teamster Billy Nicholson was also at the same pub, and finding nowhere to park left his Wolsley Drop-head and trailer slap in the middle of the rose beds!"

In the Travers trial itself Gordon had a good ride which resulted in a first class award, although as he told me he arrived at the finish with his rear tyre in a sorry state.

"On the way back to the start and finish I had a puncture in the rear tyre, but as the time was a bit tight decided to press on. As you can imagine riding with a flat was not easy, and by the time I clocked in the tyre was hanging off the rim. AMC's competition manager, Hugh Viney, took one look at it and said 'Think you could do with this Gordon' and promptly produced a new one from the back of his car!"

A rocky section at the Wye Valley Trader's trial in 1962.

For most men the long trip north and Saturday's trial would have been enough for one weekend, but not for Gordon and Johnny Giles. After arriving home in Kent at 5.00am on the Sunday morning they had three hours sleep before riding their bikes to Biggin Hill to compete in the Double Five club trial, an event won by Giles with Jackson a close second.

This sort of enthusiasm allied to Gordon's riding skills and calm, unflappable nature had certainly impressed Hugh Viney, and by the end

Gordon shows off his works AJS prior to the start of the 1962 Scottish six days.

"FOR TRIALS FANS, HIS ACHIEVEMENT OF WINNING THAT '61 SCOTTISH WITH THAT SINGLE DAB PROBABLY STANDS OUT AS HIS GREATEST RIDE"

Closely watched by Ralph Venables (right) in the 1962 Kickham.

Off-Road Giants!

of 1951 he was invited to Plumstead. Although he didn't know it at the time it would herald the start of eleven happy and highly successful seasons as an AJS works rider.

"Hugh had been watching my progress and asked me if I would like to borrow a bike for the southern Experts. It was a 500 with a 4.5:1 compression ratio and pulled like a tractor in the mud. Sadly my debut ride was rather a poor one and I finished a lowly 19th, but shortly afterwards I won the Talmag and as a result Viney told me 'you're in the team for the Victory.'"

Sadly in the trial Gordon along with several other competitors missed a section, so when Hugh Viney said 'bring your bike back' he rode up to Plumstead thinking it was possibly the end of his works ride – which was not the case, as he soon discovered.

"Standing outside the comp shop was a gleaming new 350 and I could hardly believe it when Hugh said 'take it home and try it out Gordon.' We had lots of practice sections on the farm and the new bike was simply superb, doing things that the old 500 simply wouldn't have got anywhere near."

It took all of a week for Gordon to notch up his first win on the 350, this closely followed by runner-up to Viney in the prestigious Cotswold trial, a great ride which also earned AMC's 'new boy' the 350 cup. With the works bike, 1952 proved to be a memorable year, with Jackson taking third place in his first Scottish six days and a win in the southern trial among the highlights. His close friend Johnny Giles was now mounted on Triumphs, his skill and versatility enough to earn him not only works trials and scramblers, but also a ride in the international six days trial in Austria. Two years later Gordon was also bound for Austria, and he told me about this – his first trip abroad – and his subsequent experiences in the ISDT.

"I'd first asked if I could ride in the ISDT in 1952, but my request was turned down by Hugh, who told me that AJS already had a full compliment of riders. I'd started scrambling in '53 and hoped that this might improve my chances of selection, but it would be another twelve months before I was invited to go with Hugh to compete in a three day Alpine event in Austria. Our bikes were 500cc six days twins which we loaded at Victoria, and went via Ostend and then by sleeper train to Munich; from there it was on to Austria where we rode them the last ten miles to the start. It was based in the lake-land area made famous by King Edward VIII, who took the then Mrs Simpson there prior to his abdication. Although we didn't have much chance to sit back and enjoy the views, as riding several hundred miles over rough tracks and mountain passes was hard going, both Hugh and I managed to stay on time and came away with gold medals for our efforts."

The medals unexpectedly toasted with champagne, as he told me:

"There was a long distance car trial also taking place in the same area and the competitors included Shelia Van Dam (her father ran the Windmill theatre) driving a works Sunbeam. At the end she asked us how we'd got on and after hearing of our success she ordered a magnum of champagne. 'Don't worry,' she said, 'Sir William Rootes is paying.'"

Later in the September of '54 Gordon rode the twin in the ISDT based in central Wales, but his hopes of gold were scuppered when the AJS's tank sprang a leak, and with time lost fabricating a repair he eventually finished with a silver medal. Aspirations of an International gold would never be realised, as the following year in Czechoslovakia his forks broke, leaving Gordon to concentrate on his trials and also the works 500 scrambler on which he was very competitive.

"I fancied having a go, so I asked High Viney if there was any chance of a scrambler: the answer was 'yes, but trials take preference.' After my first three races in 1953 I was upgraded to a senior – as you can imagine this was quite a rude awakening to what scrambling was all about, and it was another season before I was really on the pace."

By 1956 he was on the pace enough to be invited along with his friend Gilo to his first continental event at Lille in northern France.

The British contingent was organised by Jock Hitchcock, the Triumph agent in Folkestone who also organised the bikes and riders collection at Calais. On arrival the two young Englishmen discovered that the track was smack in the middle of the French town, and as Gordon told me their hosts encouraged them to make plenty of noise.

"When we arrived on the Saturday they were still bulldozing the big jumps, and before we went out for practice the organisers told us to 'follow that van and make as much noise as you like.'"

The sight and sound of a hoard of unsilenced bikes tearing through the cobbled streets certainly brought out the crowds, and in the 35 lap race in front of 35,000 spectators Giles brought the rasping Triumph home first, ahead of Jackson on the 500 Matchless. Gordon recalled that for this, his first continental scramble, he was paid the princely sum of £35 start money, and after expenses were accounted for he returned home with an extra £25 in his pocket, and was in his words "In heaven."

By now of course he was firmly established in the AJS line-up, and as befits a works rider had progressed to a pick-up, but like many of his contemporaries his successes and championship winning status earned him acclaim but little in the way of financial rewards.

"My day job, of course, was working on the family farm, and there was no way I could have earned enough to become a professional motorcyclist. Obviously I had free bikes, but unlike BSA, which paid its riders good retainers, AMC paid us for results. Typically this was £30 for winning a trade supported national or an extra £15 for a best in class. In real terms this ran my car or pick-up and covered my costs to compete in ordinary open to centre events, for which we weren't paid."

AMC might have been fairly tight with money, but during our conversation Gordon was quick to acknowledge the help and encouragement he received during his career and the countless friends he made along the way.

"Both my parents and my late wife Peggy who I married in 1957 were always dead keen and hugely supportive of my efforts, and many of the people I became friends with over fifty years ago are still my friends today. Motorcycling was great for that transition from boyhood into becoming a man! AJS might not have not been the greatest payer, but during my time there I was extremely well looked after and the bikes were always immaculately prepared. In my eleven Scottish six days rides they never missed a beat, although it's strange how on that last day ride to Glencoe the mind would start playing tricks and you started to hear all sorts of imaginary rattles and bangs from the motor."

Of course, it's only too easy to forget how good both the works AJS riders and their bikes were, and it's perhaps worth a reminder that in the 16 Scottish's from 1948 to 1962 Jackson and his boss Hugh Viney won no fewer that eight between them. It was on the works bike 187 BLF that Gordon achieved some of his greatest wins including the one mark Scottish in '61, so I asked him a little about that bike.

Gordon Jackson

"In an effort to keep ahead of the opposition the comp shop built up this 350cc short stroke engine and wrapped a lightweight 531 frame around it. To lighten it more they fitted narrow WD brake hubs, and Bob Mans brought it to the farm where we tested it. Unlike the earlier bike it had lots of snap which made it great in the mud, and I loved it although it wasn't as good as the long stroke Ariel on slimy rocks."

It would be Ariel-mounted Sammy Miller who was one of Gordon's greatest rivals, never more so than in the Scottish highlands where the duo fought out their annual battle for six days supremacy. So how did he become so consistent and accomplished in one of trials' greatest events?

"There's no doubt that I always had extremely competitive bikes, but I learned a lot from the quiet and unflappable Hugh Viney. Not only did he give me my first chance in the works team, something for which I was always grateful, he was also a very good tutor and taught me a lot about how important it was – especially in the Scottish – that to win you needed to be consistent and it helped to have a steady temperament."

His results alone show that Gordon Jackson was undoubtedly one of trials' all time greats, although as he revealed, his Scottish victory in 1960 carried little or no weight with the long arm of the law.

"By that time I'd pensioned off the Morris Minor pick-up and progressed to a car and trailer, but on the way back down the A1 a black Austin A70 loomed up in my mirrors and I was stopped by the police. The officer was interested in where I'd been and asked me how I'd got on. 'I won,' I said. 'Congratulations,' said the copper, 'you're nicked,' and he promptly booked me for driving the car and trailer at 55mph."

Travelling around Europe riding in both trials and scrambles inevitably brought on the odd transporter breakdown, and Gordon told me many amusing tales from these foreign escapades, tales enough to fill an article by themselves. These included memories of mending a puncture to the Morris Minor under a streetlight in northern France, and another time when he lost the bearing from his trailer wheel. After limping on to a garage forecourt the resourceful Jackson managed to cobble up a repair using a bearing from a Citroen and a forced-on aluminium nut borrowed from the trials bike, to complete his journey back to Blighty.

For trials fans, his achievement of winning that '61 Scottish with that single dab probably stands out as his greatest ride, but Gordon cites his first Scottish win in 1956 and his British Expert's victory as his personal highlights.

By 1962 Gordon and wife Peggy were running their own farm, and with this heavy workload allied to raising a young family he decided to call it a day, whereupon the famous works AJS 187 BLF passed into the hands of another Gordon, Gordon Blakeway.

It brought the curtain down on a glittering motorcycling career although it wouldn't be the last time the name of Gordon Jackson would appear as British champion.

"I told Peggy that when I retired from trials and scrambles we would do something together. She probably thought that it would be golf, so was a little surprised when I bought a trials car and she ended up as my bouncer!"

Gordon was crowned British trials car champion in 1980.

More superb action from the 1962 Scottish six days.

Bud footing his Triumph in the wet and muddy ISDT in the Isle of Man, 1965. (Photo Morton's archive)

Bud Ekins was that rarest of things – a jack of all trades but also a master of them, too. Desert racer, scrambler, long distance trials rider, dealer and stuntman, he was near the top of his profession whatever the motorcycle discipline.

CHAPTER 4
BUD EKINS - AN AMERICAN ICON

International scrambler, champion desert racer, ISDT gold medallist and Hollywood stunt rider. In a career which spanned five decades, Californian Bud Ekins was them all. He was undoubtedly one of the most talented and charismatic figures ever to throw his leg across the seat of a motorcycle, and just for good measure he also found time to open and run one of the world's largest Triumph agencies. To find out more about the man who performed perhaps the best-known motorcycle jump in the history of the movies, and who later led the American ISDT team into the hinterland of communism, I spoke to Bud at his Hollywood home. For much of both his business and racing career his name became synonymous with that of rasping Triumph twins, but as he explained, his riding began on a very different sort of machine.

"From the age of sixteen I was into hot-rod cars, and I was eighteen when I first rode a bike which my cousin had bought. I immediately loved it so went out and got one of my own; a 1934 1200cc side valve Harley Davidson. At every opportunity I would take the Harley up into the Hollywood Hills riding the dirt roads, 'cow trailing' as it was known. I got to know virtually every fire road, sand wash, mountain dirt road and desert trail in the area, and also got pretty good at sliding the bike around. My friends were impressed, and encouraged me to have a go at a hare and hounds desert race which was coming up. I didn't really know too much about it but racing against other people sounded fun so I thought I'd give it a try."

This was 1949, and from the outset Bud looked a natural. It wasn't long before he gave notice of what was to come when he notched up his first win, which he told me about.

"I'd bought this 500cc Matchless which I'd entered in the desert endurance race know as the Moose Run. I was going pretty well and fancied my chances of getting by this guy on a sprung hub Triumph; I eventually managed to overtake him on the long bumpy downhill section which led to the finish. As I crossed the line the chequered flag dropped and I'd recorded my first win."

That an 'unknown' 20 year old had won the Moose against all of the established stars was an amazing achievement, but just to prove it was no fluke Bud was soon adding to his collection of silverware. He displayed a talent for winning which brought him to the attention of local Matchless distributor Frank H Cooper who, acutely aware that a 'win on Sunday' usually secured a 'sale on Monday,' asked Bud to go work for him. He raced the Cooper Matchless in all of the important

In action in the Moose Run, which he won several times. (Photo Morton's archive)

Off-Road Giants!

On his first trip to Europe, Bud (500 Matchless) battles with Bill Baraugh's DOT on his way to 5th place in the 1952 British GP. (Photo Morton's archive)

desert races including the Big Bear, which he would later go on to win no less that three times in the 1950s. These events carried a lot of prestige, but it must be remembered that they were very different to the multi-lap scrambles found in Europe. Usually made up of two different fifty-mile loops through the desert, they frequently attracted a starting line-up well in excess of three figures, but offered little or no appeal for spectators.

As Bud told me, it was while he was working and racing for Frank that he first became aware of the motorcycle scene in the UK and scrambling on mud.

"Frank used to have the *Blue 'un [Motor Cycle]* and *Green 'un [Motorcycling]* shipped over from England and I'd read them from cover to cover. It didn't take me long to realise 'Oh boy, that's where the motorcycling is,' so Cooper made arrangements for me go to Plumstead. AMC agreed that I could have a bike to race in some end-of-season scrambles, but I had to fund the trip and all my living and travelling expenses while I was there. I went to the factory competition shop and met up with guys like Hugh Viney, Jock West and Bob Manns who I'd read about in the magazines. Manns was still very active in both one day and international six days trials, but was coming towards the end of his scrambles career, so they offered me his works bike to race. I hadn't thought how I might get the bike to the meetings so somebody suggested I should ride it. Gee, can you imagine a young guy who's never driven on the left before trying to find his way out of London on a strange motorcycle? I even got lost on the buses! Fortunately Bob Manns took pity on me and agreed to take me to the scrambles in his van."

The big man from California rode in about four events in the late summer of 1952, his all-action and never-say-die riding style soon making him a great favourite with the crowds. It whetted Bud's appetite and not surprisingly he was back the following year, this time with fellow countryman Vern E Hancock (full name Laverne Eloa Hancock).

"We both rode Matchless, but this time they were just two bikes we took off the assembly line; they weren't quite as quick and the suspension wasn't as good as the works bike, but we did OK. We were here about two months and were racing every weekend, including three or four meetings in France. What with start and prize money I was earning about £25 a week, which was good when you consider the average wage then was about £4 to £5. Jeff Ward used to deal in used cars, so we transported the bikes in an ex-RAF Standard pick-up which we rented from him for £1 a day. We also found some good digs in London. At the end of Plumstead Hill was the Royal Arsenal co-op, and behind it was an old mansion in Abbey Wood where we stayed; it cost us £3 a week including two square meals a day! People would ask us what we rode in the States and I would show 'em pictures of my bikes, they would automatically point and say 'no mudguards' to which I would reply 'no mud.'"

On returning to his native California and armed with the riding skills honed in Europe, Bud was almost unbeatable in the domestic series and was soon wearing the prestigious California 'number one' plate. Such was his dominance he would go on to win this no less than seven times, but it wasn't just the racing skills he brought back from Europe. It triggered off his association with Triumphs, opened the door to becoming a dealer, kick-started his love affair with the ISDT and also an enduring friendship with Ken Heanes.

"I was racing the Matchless at a meeting in Wales when I was overtaken on the straight by two Triumphs ridden by Johnny Gilles and Ron Stillo. I thought I would get to the 'rough bits' and catch them up but they'd all but disappeared – it was then I realised the writing was on the wall and I had to get one. I went back home and discovered that Cooper had given my job to somebody else, so I went working in my dad's welding shop. Johnson Motors was the main Triumph distributor, so I went to it and asked if they would let me have a bike. 'Yes sir you've got it,' was the reply, so from that time on I rode Triumphs; the same year (1954) I also opened up my shop."

In the sixties Bud's shop would become famous as the hangout for the famous, and he laughed as he said "If you wanted to go searching for a movie star you could either drive up and down Hollywood boulevard all day or just pull up at the back of my shop; you could usually find one or two!"

Many of Hollywood's biggest stars, including Steve McQueen, Dean Martin and Paul Newman, would become both customers and good friends of Bud's, but it took an intervention from Lady Luck to start things off.

"I was over at Meriden and happened to overhear a conversation from an executive who was saying that they'd lost their dealership in the Sacramento Valley. I approached the guy and asked if I could have the franchise to which the answer was yes! I didn't have much money, and by the time I'd sorted out some premises and got things up and running I was almost broke. Triumph was great and put all of the bikes on the forecourt and stocked me with tyres and spares. I think it took me about three years to pay 'em back. I was twenty four and probably the youngest Triumph dealer anywhere in the world."

In the passing of time he would also become one of the largest, and by the early sixties was selling 700 to 800 new bikes a year! The

Pictured at the end of Big Bear run at Fawskin 1959, Bud first – out of the 872 starters only 204 finished. (Photo Morton's archive)

"IF YOU WANTED TO GO SEARCHING FOR A MOVIE STAR YOU COULD EITHER DRIVE UP AND DOWN HOLLYWOOD BOULEVARD ALL DAY OR JUST PULL UP AT THE BACK OF MY SHOP"

On the Triumph in the Isle of Man ISDT, 1965.
(Photo Morton's archive)

Off-Road Giants!

word then in Hollywood was that if you were a star you had to have a bike, if you had a bike it must be a Triumph, and if it was a Triumph then you had to get it from Bud's!

On the California desert circuit his domination continued. In 1955 he won the prestigious Catalina Grand Prix, slicing a staggering 10 minutes off the previous race record, and in one of his Big Bear victories he completed the 153 mile course over half an hour ahead of his nearest rival. This was all despite suffering a flat tyre and damaging the rear wheel in an event which attracted nearly 1000 riders. He still found time to make visits to Europe, and he recalled racing in the Berkshire Grand National, where after pipping Ken Heanes at the post he was cruelly robbed of victory.

"There was a field of about twenty five or thirty, and by the end of the first lap I was running in about seventh place. I gradually moved up to second with just Ken Heanes ahead of me; I hung back until the last corner where I made my move and overtook. There was no time for Ken to respond and I secured what I thought was my first win in England. I was just about to celebrate when an official came up and said "I'm sorry Mr Ekins but there was a mistake with the lap scoring – you did eleven laps instead of ten so you're second."

For many of us in Europe, Bud became famous for his exploits in the international six days trial. I asked what got him interested in riding in it.

"I'd read about the ISDT in the *Blue 'un* and *Green 'un* when I was at Coopers, but it wasn't until I came to Europe and went to AMC that I realised how important it was to them. I met with Hugh Viney, Bob Manns, Ted Usher and Gordon Jackson who would be preparing all year for the September event, and several times we all went to Jacko's farm together practising. It sounded such a great event I thought that some day I'd better come back and give it a go."

With his shop up and running Bud did indeed come back and 'give it a go' at the Welsh event of 1961, although he was not the first American to ride in the ISDT. As early as 1949 fellow countryman Tommy McDermott had competed in the trial, which coincidentally was also based in Llandrindod Wells. BSA-mounted McDermott was taken under the wing of works rider Billy Nicholson, and after six days of slog was rewarded with a gold medal for his endeavours. Walt Axtheim on a Jawa and Vern Hancock also tried their best without success in the event in Austria in 1960, but for 1961 Bud was joined by Jim Brunson and Lloyd Lingelbach, who were both riding 250cc Greeves. Not surprisingly, Bud was mounted on a 650cc Triumph prepared by the comp shop at Meriden and was soon wowing the crowds with his all-action riding style. Held in superb weather, which must have reminded the big Californian of home, he was on course for gold until the last day when disaster struck.

"I was going real well, but on day six the gearbox got jammed in fourth. I had to take the outer cover off and discovered the little pawl had stuck. I clicked it back into position and was away again in twelve minutes."

Bud rode like the wind through the Welsh forest tracks in an attempt to make up for lost time but frustratingly got to the time check an agonising minute outside gold medal schedule!

"My goal had been to win an ISDT gold so I was pretty peeved to end up with silver; who knows, if I'd won gold in that first event I might not have done another one."

Not only did Bud return for the '62 event in Garmisch-Partenkirchen, he did so in some style, winning not only his sought-after gold but also finishing first in the hotly contested 750cc class, beating the entire factory BMWs in the process.

It was during this time that he added to his impressive resume of shop owner, desert racer and ISDT star that of stunt rider, when he joined his great pal Steve McQueen in the filming of *The Great Escape*. It would also trigger off events which would lead to America's first team entry in the East German six days of '64; a team which would comprise Bud (captain), his younger brother Dave Ekins, Steve McQueen, Cliff Coleman and reserve John Steen. I started by asking Bud about that famous leap for freedom, a jump which is often wrongly attributed to McQueen.

"Steve was in Germany filming *The Great Escape* when I got this letter inviting me over to perform some motorcycle stunts which the insurance people wouldn't allow him to do. At that time he was one of Hollywood's biggest stars so you can imagine the repercussions if he'd injured himself and been laid up for three or four months. It was perfect timing for me because the ISDT was coming up, so it meant I could go to Europe and take a break during the filming to ride in the trial. I was five inches taller than Steve, but they cut and bleached my hair and dressed me in the same style clothes so you couldn't tell the difference. The bike was a stock '62 Triumph which weighed in at about 400lb. I jumped a distance of sixty five feet over the 12 foot high wire and all the filming was done in just one pass; I've got a feeling it was the first thousand dollar movie stunt."

Between shooting a lot of bike talk took place, especially regarding the six days trial, and by the time filming was completed McQueen was converted into competing in the 'motorcycling Olympics.' By virtue of their victory in Czechoslovakia the previous year the honour of hosting the '64 trial fell to the East Germans, so I asked Bud what he remembers about the preparation for the event.

"Steve was perhaps the least experienced of our team, but he was incredibly enthusiastic and he spent a lot of time practising and racing in desert events. He was a very useful rider and after completing *The Great Escape* he took the whole year off preparing himself for the ISDT, including coming to work in my shop. Much of the time he was there he was changing tyres, and got so quick he could do one on a Triumph in about four minutes."

The Americans were to be mounted on Triumphs and came to England to practise ahead of the September event, enlisting British team captain Ken Heanes in their preparations. Bud's team-mates had little or no experience of racing on mud, so Ken took them to central Wales where they found plenty. After demonstrating how to negotiate a typical Welsh bog Ken waved Steve forward to have a go. He hit the mud at high speed and promptly disappeared over the handlebars. Covered from head to toe in green slime he got up with a big cheesy grin and said "Gee, do you think you could show me that again Ken?"

The machines were short of the specification of those supplied to the British team and were taken to Comerfords at Thames Ditton, where the Americans were given free reign of the workshops. With fettling and improvements carried out they set forth in the 'Club America' van which team manager Ted Wassel had secured from Triumph dealers H&L motors; Wassel following closely behind in his Jaguar car. All went well until they arrived at the heavily guarded border post, and Bud takes up the story again.

"When we got to the East German border we were held up for

Bud Ekins - an American icon

about four hours while they checked our passports. Remember this was at the height of the Cold War and it wasn't everyday they had Americans wanting to enter, especially when one of them was a big Hollywood star. I think they had to phone Berlin to make sure that Steve had never made any anti-Communist movies before they let us through. We had to pass through about four miles of no man's land and were given strict instructions of 'no stopping and no photographs.'"

Despite their lack of ISDT experience the American team performed extremely well, and by end of day three they were all on gold medal schedule and leading the silver vase class. Sadly, on day four both Steve and Bud suffered crashes, and although Bud managed to get to the finish he was diagnosed with a broken ankle, and with McQueen's bike too badly damaged to continue both men had to retire. Although the team were out of contention Dave Ekins and Cliff Coleman each went on to win gold and John Steen silver.

The story of Hollywood behind the Iron Curtain is well documented in Sean Kelly's book *40 Summers Ago*, and during the course of our conversation Bud told me enough tales to fill another volume. Stories of MZs being overhauled in a van, minders waiting in woods, and a route marking system that favoured the home team will have to wait until another time, as I was intrigued to know how Kelly's book came about.

"A girlfriend of Sean's is a neighbour of mine, and one day she offered to sort out some of my stuff for me including my boxes of photos which were all jammed under my pool table. She was sticking them into albums when Sean happened to come by and saw a photo with McQueen sat on his ISDT Triumph. With a magnifying glass Kelly could read the engine number and after a lot of detective work discovered that the bike still existed. Not only did he manage to buy the bike from its then owner Frank Danielson in Sacramento, the photograph albums triggered off the idea of recording the '64 ISDT to print."

Throughout the sixties Bud continued to ride in the six days trial, and after the disappointment of a DNF in the waterlogged Isle of Man event of '65 he added to his collection of golds in Sweden in 1966, and the following year in Poland. By now the heavyweight Triumph twins were no longer competitive, and Bud had moved on to 2-stroke Husqvarnas. He continued to balance stunt work with running his shop and desert enduros, and was a founder member of the Baja 1000 race down the Mexican peninsula. One of his greatest rivals was a young Eddie Mulder who sensationally won the Big Bear aged only seventeen. Bud had been in the lead when his bike expired, but when questioned by a reporter he was philosophical about the situation and drawled "Hell, I was on my third cigarette before Mulder came by."

After the best part of twenty years of top class racing Bud hung up his leathers, sold the shop and concentrated on stunt riding. Needless to say, given his pedigree he became one of Hollywood's best. If you've ever seen the film *Bullit* then Bud was the rider who laid the bike down under the truck, and he was also the driver of the Ford Mustang. He eventually retired from stunts in 1997 and since then concentrated his energies on restoring his ever burgeoning collection of motorcycles; all of which got regularly ridden 'cow trailing' along those favourite dirt roads in the Hollywood hills.

Bud was undoubtedly one of motorcycling's great characters, and it was a privilege to spend some time talking to him. He passed away in October 2007, and the friendship with Ken Heanes which started at Aldworth and the Berks GN in '55 endured over fifty years.

Bud in action on the Husqvarna on the first day of the 1966 ISDT in Sweden. (Photo Morton's archive)

Jerry Scott on his 500 Cheney BSA at Leighton Frome in 1965.

CHAPTER 5

The Cheney name was synonymous with off-road success in the sixties and seventies, and attracted a whole host of top class riders to compete in scrambles and international six days trials on their beautifully-crafted machines.

CHENEY HISTORY AND THE BUSINESS TODAY

At the edge of a quiet cul-de-sac in the leafy suburbs of Fleet in Hampshire lies the Potters industrial estate, which to the uninitiated is little different from scores of similar business estates found the length and breadth of the country. However, behind the face of a rather nondescript grey door is the home of Inter-Moto and the name that for half a century has reverberated around the motocross tracks of the world: Cheney.

The business was founded by Eric Cheney in 1961, and the site at Potters has been the company's home for the last 20 years. It is now run by Eric's son, Simon, and dotted around its walls are pictures and mementos of some of their glories and achievements; these include Eric in the south versus north scramble team of 1951, and a large autographed action photo of ex-world champion Jeff Smith.

Although they are healthy reminders of the past the workshop bristles with the present, and is jammed to the rafters with everything from bare molybdenum tubing awaiting forming through to a gleaming – recently restored – Aberg replica motocrosser.

Having won the 250 and 500cc British classic motocross championships three years on the trot from 1998 to 2000, Simon has earned an enviable reputation as a racer of the highest pedigree. It's certainly a case of 'a chip off the old block,' as during the 1950s his father became one of the best known scramblers of his generation. Eric was still in the navy when his racing career began in 1946, on an army surplus 350cc Triumph that he'd repatriated from Egypt. Already it was no ordinary bike, as he had removed the original girder forks and replaced them with telescopics from a Matchless. By 1947 Eric was working for Homesteads, the local Triumph agent, and had progressed to an alloy-engined 500cc VCH Ariel. This bike was soon given the 'Cheney touch,' and, at a time when most scrambles machines were equipped with girder forks and rigid rear ends, Eric's featured telescopic forks and a McCandless rear swinging arm conversion which gave four inches of suspension movement. This was before Artie Bell and Rex McCandless moved to England, so for a rider who wanted one of his trendsetting conversions the whole frame had to be dispatched to Ireland, for which turnaround was usually three weeks. In the 'pre-Girling' days, the conversion included the fitment of a copy of the shock absorbers normally fitted to Jeeps, which, when used in the rigours of scrambling, constantly blew seals.

1950 was a memorable year for Eric when aboard his Ariel he won both the Sunbeam point–to-point and the Hants Grand National.

Eric on the Ariel with the McCandless rear swinging arm in 1948.
(Photo Cheney archive)

Eric aviates his Ariel at Cadwell Park in 1952.
(Photo Cheney archive)

Off-Road Giants!

Keith Hickman on his Cheney BSA at Chard in 1964.

His reward was a works machine from Selly Oak and selection for the Motocross Des Nations team in Sweden, and again the following year at Namur in Belgium. It was also the year which first saw Eric compete on 'foreign soil' in an event at Montrieul near Paris, for which he was paid the handsome start fee of £70. It has now been built over, but at the time it was a very famous circuit in a chalk pit and featured a drop called the 'grand descent'; a fearsome jump of some twenty feet from the summit.

From as early as 1948/49 top calibre riders like Basil Hall and Harold Lines had latched on to the lucrative money to be earned from racing on the continent, and for the next ten years it would be a way of life for Eric. He was by now working for Archers in nearby Aldershot, and from 1952 onwards raced in the company of his friend Les Archer on a brace of Nortons, in what was in effect the works scrambles team. The bikes, which featured SOHC Manx engines and a highly modified featherbed frame, were steadily developed, and by 1956 were good enough for Les to win the coveted 500cc European championship (the fore runner to the world championship). To accommodate the 21in wheel, the frames – which were Bracebridge street castoffs – were cut and a bow introduced to the front downtubes, and at the rear the twin top tubes were removed at the gusset plate and replaced by a single tube.

It is perhaps difficult to comprehend the weight of these mighty 4-strokes and the strength and skill they took to ride. To give you an example, the Archer/Cheney Nortons – which turned out about 36 horsepower – tipped the scales at 330lb with a 500cc Goldie weighing in a few pounds more. All of the development work with Les proved to be very much an 'apprenticeship' for Eric, and eventually in 1960 he manufactured his first complete frame which was wrapped around a 500cc AJS pushrod engine. This was a watershed, as not only was it the first Cheney, it also broke the hitherto magical 300lb barrier when it weighed in at 295lb. The bike was later sold to Ken Cleghorn who took it to New Zealand to win the Kiwi's winter championship, and to my knowledge it still resides there to this day.

Eric continued to race on the continent, but in 1961 while competing in Algeria he picked up a blood infection, and after a prolonged illness was forced to retire to concentrate on engine preparation and frame building. From the workshop at the rear of his home Eric set to, and with no racing to distract him soon made the motocross world sit up and take notice with the Gold Star he created for the talented Jerry Scott. The bike, which carried its oil in the frame, featured an engine fitted with magnesium engine and gearbox castings, and shaved a staggering 50lb off the previously ponderous Goldie. Fitted with Ceriani forks, a skimmed Matchless front hub, and a petrol tank resplendent in anodised blue, it looked a thing of beauty. Ridden by the impressive Scott it notched up numerous victories during the 1963 TV scrambles series and the British championship rounds, but despite these wins the writing was on the wall and the era of Goldie dominance was coming to an end. Jeff Smith was achieving remarkable results on the factories lightweight unit construction singles, and it would trigger the next phase of development for Cheney. Eric was held in high esteem within the walls of BSA, and despite (or perhaps because of) losing his star rider Scott to Small Heath he received one of the 420cc singles known as 'Black Bess' from the BSA comp shop, which was

In typical forceful action, Simon on his BSA-engined bike. (Photo Cheney archive)

Simon on his way to victory in France in 1997.
(Photo Cheney archive)

Off-Road Giants!

then housed in his own frame and raced by his new recruit Keith Hickman.

Hickman carried the name of Cheney into the GPs, and the quality of both the bike and the rider were evident at the opening round of the 1965 season in Austria, when Hickman brought the victor home in fourth place. These were exciting days for the little concern from Hampshire, and would be the prelude to the rest of the decade as they harried and often beat the 'Goliaths' of the motocross world, but were constantly denied that deserved Grand Prix victory.

For Simon – who was born in 1959 – accompanying his parents around the motocross tracks of the world became a way of life, so I asked him how his own motorcycle career started.

"Dad wouldn't allow me to ride in schoolboy scrambles as he figured that my body would suffer in later life, so my competition career started at the age of ten in the gentle art of trials riding. My first event was a local club trial at Cranston's pit on a Triumph Tiger cub which we'd bought from dad's old mate Les Archer. It was little more than a modified road bike and had extremely poor ground clearance. On the approach to section one there was a bump which immediately showed up the baby Triumphs limitations. It grounded and I was left rocking, unable to move forward and reach the first section; the trial for me was over before it started. Dad helped me get it off and I just rode around for the rest of the day without tackling the sections!"

By 1970 the burgeoning business had outgrown the workshop behind the family home and moved to the old tobacco drying factory at Redfield's. Eric's machines had built up a reputation for both their quality and durability, and it came as no surprise when he was commissioned by the ACU to construct eight Triumph-engined bikes for the 45th ISDT in Spain. Despite first day problems which saw John Pease plagued by punctures and John Giles suffer a split petrol tank, all the trophy bikes kept going to the finish. Not only did the 504cc bikes keep going, they revelled in the motocross track special tests, and the British trio of Jim Sandiford, Bill Wilkinson and team captain Ken Heanes led the half-litre and above class to the end, beating the much fancied BMW-mounted West German team in the process.

These were heady days for Cheney, but not so for some of the British industries major players, and BSA was on the edge of the abyss. In July 1972 the comp shop was disbanded, leaving what was possibly Britain's finest squad of motocross GP riders without a ride. Among them was John Banks who had twice been runner-up in the world championship, and after a brief foray onto CZ 2-strokes he agreed to ride for Cheney in the 1973 season. It had been Eric's burning ambition to see a Cheney-mounted rider at the top of a GP rostrum, and during that memorable '73 season his dream was almost realised. Banks put in a series of blistering rides including a second at Carlsbad in America, where he split the works Suzukis of De Coster and Wolsink. However, that coveted GP win eluded him and he had to be content with Banks becoming British 500cc champion, and as history would record the last to achieve this on a British bike.

The success generated by John Banks spawned a huge amount of interest from customers wanting replicas, and the workshop was running flat out trying to satisfy demand. In addition to making the stunningly beautiful JBRs, Cheney was also supplying frame kits to former ISDT captain and dealer Ken Heanes. Ken had seen a commercial opportunity to make a clubman's motocross machine, and negotiated a deal with BSA to supply B50 motocross engines wheels and forks which he would assemble into the Cheney frames and sell as Heanes Thumpers. The initial plan was for 500 machines to be made, but these were very troubled times for BSA, and for whatever reason only about 125 actually made it into production.

With trade buoyant, Eric moved his business and workforce, which now numbered around a dozen, to new premises near Fleet station in 1974. Four of these staff were involved in milling and machining, four welding, three on assembly, plus Eric and three part timers. It soon became a 'bakers dozen' when Simon joined them after leaving school in 1975, and I asked him how his own riding career had developed.

"After the less than encouraging start on the Tiger Cub I was now riding regularly in trials, initially on a Whithawk Bantam which had the exhaust pipe running through the frame, and then onto Ossa's. Although most of dad's work revolved around motocross bikes he diversified into a lot of other projects, including making cantilever Ossa frames for John Holden. We did a lot of the development work which involved experimenting with different head angles and various pivot points and suspension setups for the rear end. I then rode these mobile test beds in one day trials and also in a lot of time trials, which were very popular at the time. Not only did it improve my balance and control, it also built up my speed, stamina and fitness for when I started scrambling, which was on a 500cc JBR at a Boxing Day meeting near Fair Oak in 1976. The only thing that sticks in my mind was that I fell off rather a lot, which had nothing to do with too much Christmas revelry. After six months racing on the JBR I'd won enough points to be upgraded to an Expert, and I managed to get a few wins at centre level and also rode a few times in France. The 500cc JBR was a fantastic bike to ride, but dad was never one for standing still and it soon developed into the machine that was ridden by Bent Aberg."

Nowadays it's only too easy to associate Cheney's with just using British 4-stroke engines for motive power, but this was far from being the case, as Simon explained.

"Dad was not a great one for keeping records so I don't know how many bikes were built in the early years, but we used all sorts of engines many of which were one-offs, including the water-cooled Husky that did away with a radiator and carried its coolant in the frame. We also used both 2- and 4-stroke Yamaha engines and developed our own leading link front forks and rear single shock suspension system."

Most of the contemporary monoshock systems used a variety of rods, levers and rocker arms, but the Cheney version dispensed with these and relied on one using just three pivot points. Fitted with this system and the leading link front forks the Yamaha gave an incredible 13in of suspension movement – light years from Eric's old Ariel.

Something that Simon remembers with great fondness is the 20 or so cantilever-framed XL 250/350 Hondas they made.

"Chris Scrivens knew a thing or two about Hondas and rode one in the UK, and we sold a batch to SDVL in France. They featured a cantilever frame with two shocks mounted under the saddle, and ready to race only weighed about 236lb. They were in a fairly soft state of tune but handled exceptionally well, and in France won first time out. A small batch went to the USA where the 350 was fitted with a Powroll piston and stroker kit, which gave a displacement of 440cc and was probably the most powerful 500cc 4-stroke we ever built.

I was doing most of our development work on the track, which

Cheney history and the business today

was interesting but also very frustrating as often I was thwarted by niggling little problems during a race."

All of the major manufacturers were now producing bikes that handled and won straight from the crate, so the tide had turned on the little constructor from Fleet, so much so that by the late '70s Cheney's was forced to downsize and relocate its operations, initially to a workshop at Eric's sisters and then in 1984 to the present site at Potters industrial estate. Simon had also become somewhat disillusioned, and worked for a while at Les Archers sports cars and then for County tractors before rejoining his father again in 1984. Simon takes up the story again:

"There was less and less work on the motocross bikes but we managed to diversify into a range of other projects, including several for the army. These included the construction of a rolling chassis for a diesel bike and the manufacture of a disc braked leading link front end for a Rotax. We experienced lots of fuelling problems with the diesel engine, which had a 15:1 compression ratio and had a habit of lifting the barrel securing studs from the crankcase. The army ended up making a rolling road so they could get it started. The Rotax bike featured a single sided rear swinging arm, and we made the leading link front forks that slid straight into the standard yolks. When it was finished the man from the military came down and wanted to be shown how much better it was than standard. I rode it over a pile of pallets and they seemed impressed but took it away and it was the last we heard of it. With all of the army projects we had to sign the official secrets act, but this was a waste of time as dad put little on paper and carried virtually everything in his head.

We did other things like the cantilever-framed XT 250 trials bike and a complete pre-production machine for Brooklands motorcycles. This was an interesting but still-born project which used a Rotax engine housed in a replica Manx Norton frame, but it wasn't until the classic scrambles scene came about that we saw an upturn in business. Suddenly scores of people had an interest in the old bikes again, and an increasing amount wanted them restored or converted back to their original specification. As classic racing took off it also kick-started my own racing career back into action."

After suffering a mild heart attack at work in August of 2001 complications set in, and sadly Eric died in hospital on 30th of December, 2001. It was the first time he'd seen a doctor in 33 years.

Today with the workshop continuously busy the business has come virtually full circle, and Simon gets little opportunity to compete regularly himself. In fact, when he raced at a meeting near Toulouse in September 2003 it was the first time he'd ridden for nearly two years. Despite the scorching heat which saw temperatures nudging 100 degrees, Simon showed that he'd lost little of his dashing style and won both of his races on the booming Cheney victor.

Times have changed, but the lovingly crafted products from the 'House of Cheney' live on across the race tracks of the world, and are a permanent reminder of a man with a dream, Eric Cheney.

Chris on the Rickman-framed Matchless in the 1965 national Cotswold scramble.

When Chris Horsfield went to his first scramble he vowed that within three years he'd be a professional racer. In fact, he would become one of the best scramblers of his generation, who, with a bit of luck, could have been a world champion.

CHAPTER 6
CHRIS HORSFIELD

The scene is the Russian steppes in the early summer of 1966. The lights from a hundred campfires glint out across the endlessly flat landscape and the sound of singing drifts on the clear summer air. A huge caravan of gipsies has pulled up for the night and their camp is alive with dancing and the aroma of freshly cooking food. Among the travellers are four faces that are unmistakably those of 'foreigners', two Brits and two Swedes.

You might be forgiven for thinking it's a plot from a spy film. However, the Romany's guests are not secret agents, but a quartet of international motocross riders; Chris Horsfield, Jerry Scott, Rolph Tiblin and his fellow countryman Per-Olaf Persson. They are en route to the Russian Motocross GP, and frustrated by their Soviet minders' sluggardly rate of progress, have decided to press on independently. Remember it's the height of the Cold War, so four westerners on their own behind the Iron Curtain is almost enough to trigger an international incident! The roads across the barren steppes are straight and boring, so faced with a dearth of a suitable cafés and hotels they opted to join the surprised gipsy folk; a meal of roast goat and a night under the stars the reward for Horsfield and co. Chris laughed as he recalled the incident although it was tinged with some sadness as a few weeks later his close friend and travelling companion Jerry Scott was tragically killed while racing in the North V South scramble at Thirsk.

By '66 CZ-mounted Chris had become an established works rider and – courtesy of his success in the Grandstand and World of Sport TV scrambles – a household name. I was keen to find out more about the life of this professional motocrosser who, in a quest for world championship honours, spent five months of the year travelling the roads of Europe, but also about those early days before he became famous.

His racing career started in 1957 on a BSA B32 although, as I discovered, racing motorbikes was not Chris' first ambition.

"I was brought up in the era of great racing drivers like Fangio, and as a young boy dreamed of following in his footsteps. My mother and father were friendly with the Moss family and I remember a fantastic day when we were all invited along to Silverstone where Stirling and Mike Hawthorn were testing. In his yellow polka dot Dickie bow Mike Hawthorn was a great character and as I soon discovered a great practical joker, especially where Moss was concerned. Stirling came back into the pits and said he couldn't believe how narrow the track seemed in the area controlled by cones; but what he didn't know was

An early outing on the works 250cc James at Bridport in 1962.

"THEY ARE EN ROUTE TO THE RUSSIAN MOTOCROSS GP, AND FRUSTRATED BY THEIR SOVIET MINDERS' SLUGGARDLY RATE OF PROGRESS, HAVE DECIDED TO PRESS ON INDEPENDENTLY"

Dicing with John Harris at Yarley in 1963.

Off-Road Giants!

that Hawthorn had been closing them up and before he (Moss) had pitted he'd opened them up again. Moss said that the car was so easy to drive a kid could do it so Mike, who scoffed at the notion, wagered him £10 on it; as I was the only kid I was stuck behind the wheel of the Formula One car, and on my first ever drive won Moss the bet! I told him I wanted to become a racing driver but his answer was 'forget it unless you've got plenty of money.' It was then I decided I would opt for two wheels instead of four."

The young Chris soon became the proud owner of an old James, a machine on which he learnt the art of off-road control although it also earned him a ticking off from the long arm of the law.

"I was fourteen and was riding the James through the lanes to the fields. Normally this was fine, but one day I came upon a police roadblock; somebody had done a runner from the nearby asylum and they were out looking for him. It was obvious I wasn't old enough to be on the road so they turned me round and followed me back home in the police car. I thought I would be nicked but because they'd told me to ride it home it would have been seen as aiding and abetting, so I was let off with some finger wagging and a stern lecture."

At sixteen Chris started work on a farm and the James was pensioned off, the little 2-stroke replaced by a B31 BSA which he rode to watch his first scramble.

"Rob, Sam Cooper and I went to watch the scramble at Knowlsworth, a top line event which featured people like John Draper, Geoff Ward, Brian Stonebridge and a young chap called Jeff Smith, I just couldn't believe how fast they were going. It was there and then I decided to be a scrambler, although Sam and Rob thought that I was joking when I said I gave myself three years to become a professional rider. It's not surprising that they laughed, because at that time there were very few able to earn a living wage from racing motorbikes."

Remember at this stage Chris had never even sat on a scrambler let alone ridden one, but not to be deterred he soon had his first bike, a BSA B32 which he recalled cost £150.

"The BSA dealer in Stratford was surprised when I told him I wanted to buy the B32, and kept reminding me that it was a competition bike and I wouldn't be able to ride it on the road. I couldn't kick it over, let alone start it, but when he realised I was serious he allowed me £30 on the B31 and the rest I took up on higher purchase at £1 a month."

In his state of 'must have it' Chris had given little consideration to how he might get the Goldie home, so with no transport available the only option was to push it the three and a half miles from the centre of Stratford!

It transpired that the Goldie had previously been raced by Ron Langston, so it was an optimistic Chris who, in 1957, lined up for his first race.

"The Cooper brothers and I had decided to pool our resources and we'd bought an ex-army A40 pick-up truck. It was a bit of a heap and before we could drive it away we had to weld the doors up – this meant that the only way to get in was through the windows! We then discovered that of its three gears it was only first and top which selected, but amazingly it got us to my first meeting at Kimber Edge near Stourbridge."

After he disappeared through a hedge Chris' debut race ended in retirement. However, on his second outing of the afternoon he gave a hint of his potential when he brought the Goldie home fifth in a race won by Bull Baraugh on the works DOT.

"I rode in about five events during the latter half of '57 and I fell off more than I stayed on. It was certainly a lot harder than I could possibly have imagined."

Farm workers' pay was pitifully poor, and for Chris it was hard to finance his passion for scrambling. His 5/s entry fee, petrol and bike upkeep all had to be paid for by a weekly wage of £3. It probably comes as little surprise to learn that by 1958, he had left the farm and was working in a local garage run by the Bollom family; the change of vocation hastened when he crashed his former employer's tractor though a hedge.

He was getting on the pace, but due to its huge carburettor the Goldie had little in the way of bottom end power. Once under way it went like the wind, but invariably Chris was last away which meant playing catch up; youthful over-exuberance resulting in an almost inevitable crash. 1958 was an eventful year and for much of the time he was either dicing for the lead or falling off, but as he told me, a new bike soon brought its rewards the following season.

"If I was going to reach my three year goal of becoming a works rider I had to have a decent bike or pack up. I decided to put my money where my mouth was and bought myself a brand new B34 Gold Star, which cost a whopping £378. I soon started winning and it was a fantastic year for prize money and silverware. By then I was travelling to events as far afield as Derbyshire and Wales in a shared van with Bonzo Harris and Terry Player, who acted as mechanic."

From his earliest days Chris has kept carefully chronicled records of his career, and they reveal that in that '59 season he was winning about £30 a week in prize money – a decent return when you consider the average wage was then about £10! His riding ability was starting to get him noticed and he was chosen to compete in the annual Oxford versus Cambridge scramble.

"It was a great honour to be chosen for the Oxford side. I had a good event and although I didn't win I managed to beat Brian Stonebridge – but remember that he was riding a 197cc Greeves and I was on a 500cc BSA. I'd been racing two and a half seasons and really thought I'd made it but was brought down to earth the following year. 1960 turned out to be a bit of a nightmare and I was forever crashing, one was so bad it bent the Goldie's frame. It needed replacing so we stripped it down and my dad took it on the bus to BSA's where competition chief Bert Perigo gave him a new one."

He soon returned to his winning ways and attracted the eyes of a sponsor.

"A chap in Coventry invited me to ride a TriBSA and a Greeves Hawkestone which was my first 2-stroke. I just couldn't get on with the power delivery of the Triumph twin engine and only rode it once. I landed from a jump and the jolt must have done something to the carb, because when I shut the throttle back it was spitting so badly it caught fire and I had to bale off at around 50mph."

He may not have liked the TriBSA but he took to the little Greeves like a duck to water. On his first outing he won a snowy TV scramble in Derbyshire, although getting to the venue was not without its problems.

"Bob and Sam were due to pick me up at 6.00am on the Saturday morning, but overnight there had been a heavy snowfall so the lane to my village was impassable. I loaded up my kit bag and started pushing the Greeves but the drifts were too deep, so the only option was to start it. It was fitted with one of those flat megaphones, so as you can

At the Hants Grand National, Easter 1963.

One of Chris' first rides on the works 500cc Matchless in 1963.

Off-Road Giants!

imagine it was horrendously noisy riding it through the village. We eventually loaded up, but the A40 didn't have a heater, and because of the treacherous going we only arrived in time to do one lap of practice; despite this I quickly adapted to the snow and surprised myself by winning the first TV race."

Sadly, before he could taste the fruit of further success the sponsor went bust, so once more Chris was without a bike to ride. This was short-lived and soon he was lined up to ride the ex-Ron Langston works Ariel, a bike bought by Bert Lavis after Langston had retired with a back injury.

"My first event on the Ariel was another TV scramble and it was a revelation after my Gold Star, it was light and went like a rocket ship although it didn't handle as well as the BSA. The peaty going was just to my liking, and in the race I finished second to Jeff Smith."

It was one of Smith's first races against the young Horsfield, and on arrival back in the pits he is reported to have asked 'who is that mad little bugger?'

Again the association with the Ariel was short lived – after four or five races Chris landed from a jump and on impact the frame broke in half.

"It split at the head and I cartwheeled down the track – I've still got the tyre marks on my back to prove it. It went back to Selly Oak to have a new frame fitted, but while it was there they took out all of the 'good bits' so on its return it was just a stock and rather uncompetitive bike."

For a while Chris considered retiring, but again lady luck intervened in the form of Norman Houghton. Norman was the then competition manager for Lodge plugs, and invited Chris to ride and help develop a bike he was involved in. After meeting Norman Chris agreed to ride the bike, although at that stage it hadn't even been built!

"A few weeks later I got a call to say that it was ready, so the first time I actually saw the bike was on the Sunday I turned up to race it. It had a 197cc Villiers engine, a small section 3.50 rear tyre, and looked more like a road bike than a scrambler! I raced it two or three times but it was absolutely dreadful. Then out of the blue I got a phone call from Bob Bicknell who was the sales manager for James and Francis Barnett. He told me there was a position available at James and it was mine if I was interested. I was still working in the garage on a wage of about £7 a week so James' offer of £11 seemed like riches in comparison. It involved a daily round trip of 40 miles, but I decided to take it."

Chris spent the first two weeks working in the underground workshop building wheels, welding and road testing, but he then got a call to go to the comp shop. James had been hoping to sign Sammy Miller to help develop the Commando trials bike but for reasons unclear this didn't happen, so Chris was invited to develop and ride the scrambler.

"I was working with Eddie Kees who was a brilliant mechanic and could make virtually anything. Two-stroke tuning was still a bit of an unknown art so we experimented with the Villiers engine, padding the crankcases and fitting a Parkinson conversion which got it going really well. Although we didn't realise it at the time it was the infancy of the Starmaker engine."

Much to their surprise Chris and the James started winning, although between races the bike was totally stripped and rebuilt for the following weekend. And it turned out it wasn't just the bike that was stripped down!

"The James machine shop was largely run by women and like something out of the 1930s, with huge machines driven by exposed belts. I was starting to get some good results and on my way to the comp shop the women would sometime whistle or shout out, however one day I was aware that the whole room had an eerie quietness about it. Before I knew what was happening I was surrounded by a group of baying women who proceeded to strip all my clothes off, and I had to run naked to the safety of the comp shop – needless to say, I didn't go that way again!"

Chris was perhaps not the most naturally gifted rider, but what he lacked in skill was more than made up for in stamina, and a typical day involved a 3½ mile run before he started work. He might have been a works rider but he still had to clock in at 8 o'clock every morning!

He was soon on the trail of the continental GPs but his championship ambitions met with little enthusiasm from his employers.

"We got the twin carb'd-engined James going really well, so I thought that the GPs were the natural progression, but when I asked they said 'don't know, you'll have to pay for it yourself.' So I went ahead and managed to get a ride in the 1962 Swiss GP, my first trip abroad. Although I had to pay for it myself they let Bob Cooper go as my mechanic, and we made the long two and a half day trip to Payerne along with journalist Chris Carter. Our 'race transport' was an old Ford Thames van which I bought for 30 quid, and this also acted as our overnight accommodation."

At that time Chris was an unknown outside the UK, although at the impromptu pre-race party he became the centre of attention.

"Jan was expecting our first child, and after about four laps of practice I was pulled off the track to receive a telegram announcing that Grant had been born. The Russians and Czechs threw a massive party to celebrate and with the help of Sten Lundin and Andy Lee, I eventually managed to send a return telegram."

In the race Chris also did rather well and finished a creditable fifth, despite having to ride half the race without a seat. His employers may not have given much in the way of encouragement or support for his trip to Payerne, but later they sold 80 bikes to the Swiss importer as a result of his success!

Throughout his career Chris had suffered a number of heavy crashes, but undoubtedly the one at Hawkstone in late '62 was the worst.

"Although the James didn't handle as well as the Greeves or BSA opposition, the Starmaker engine was very quick, and I was involved in a dice for the lead with Jeff Smith. We came out of the sandpit absolutely flat out onto the straight and the next thing I remember was waking up in a hospital bed. Apparently I got flipped off and collided with the fencing; it resulted in bruising to the brain and I had to stay in a darkened room for about 6 weeks."

Not to be deterred, Chris was soon back in the saddle although this time on a booming 500cc Matchless.

"Dave Curtis was retiring so they asked me if I'd like to take over his bike. As you can guess the answer was 'blimey yeah!' I think Hugh Viney looked upon it as his baby, and before my first ride at Rolsworth he gave me strict instructions of 'don't crash and don't damage it!' It didn't handle particularly well, but the engine turned out the best part of 50bhp so it was an absolute rocket ship, good for close on 100mph."

In addition to Dave Curtis, Geoff Ward and Gordon Blakeway were also coming to the end of their careers, so Chris joined a new team which comprised himself, Vic Eastwood and Dave Nichol to fly

At the Hants GN in Easter 1964.

"BEFORE I KNEW WHAT WAS HAPPENING I WAS SURROUNDED BY A GROUP OF BAYING WOMEN WHO PROCEEDED TO STRIP ALL MY CLOTHES OFF"

Leading the Minety Vale motocross in August 1964.

Off-Road Giants!

the Matchless flag. It was something which for the next three years he achieved with great aplomb, although Viney was ever watchful – after one race Chris found a note pinned to the bike which read 'change up or else!'

"They were fantastic days, although riding in the GPs was very demanding. The season started in Austria and then went on to Monza in Italy; from there we would drive all the way up to Finland, Sweden, Denmark and Germany before coming home for six weeks. It might sound romantic, but we had to drive thousands of miles and between races had to do all our own maintenance on the bikes, and keep to our training schedule."

However, it was not all work and no play for the Brit's chasing world championship honours, and they did find time to let their hair down.

"After we'd raced in the Austrian GP we met an old guy who'd fought in the war but was now keen to celebrate peace and friendship with his former 'enemies'. A group of us including Jerry Scott and myself were invited to his home which, as it happened, had a room licensed to sell home-brewed wine and liquor. Around the room ran a dado rail, and after a few (read many) glasses of schnapps the Austrian displayed his party trick of running around it. By this time it was two o'clock in the morning and we'd all partied well, but none of us, including Jerry or myself, could manage it; this was particularly frustrating because the Austrian was eighty if he was a day. I think it was another twenty years or more before I could face another glass of red wine!"

The works Matchless was in Chris' words "like a rocket ship," but compared to the opposition massively heavy, and the rider's request to lighten things fell on deaf ears with Hugh Viney. However, away from the bosses' prying eyes things did get done.

"A resourceful group of ex-Norton comp shop old boys joined us from Bracebridge Street, and no job was ever too much trouble or too difficult for them. We had special innards made for the front forks, electron brake plates, lightweight rockers and a clutch turned out of a solid billet of aircraft alloy. It shaved an amazing 7lb off the weight of the standard clutch, which had been struggling to deal with the engine's huge torque; it made the world of difference and when married up to a lightweight Swedish gearbox the bike fairly flew."

There was no disputing the bike's performance, but around the paddocks there were murmurings that after its visits to the comp shop the half-litre single's displacement sometimes 'grew' an extra 100cc – rumours which always led to tight-lipped denial from comp shop bosses and were never proven.

Certainly the Grand Prix riders were a close-knit crowd, and during the long season would often play host to their on-track rivals between races, help with some chores the usual 'payment' – although as Chris recalled, this was not the case in Sweden.

"We'd ridden in Finland – where I was horrified to pay £4 10s for breakfast – and before the Swedish round Rolf Tiblin invited me, Jerry Scott and his father Len to stay at his (Rolf's) family's home in Stockholm. Tiblin senior was a scrap metal man and told us that anyone who stayed in his house was welcome but was expected to work for their keep. I wasn't sure what he had in mind but we were woken at 5.30 in the morning and after breakfast put in a really long, hard day helping him to dismantle a huge road bridge over Stockholm harbour."

Ernie Wiffin had taken over as competition manager from Hugh Viney, but all was not well with the AMC parent company and Chris was given the tip-off that he should start looking around for another ride.

This was the back end of 1964, and BSA was celebrating Jeff Smiths 500cc world championship win on the lightweight 440 victor. It was a machine ideally suited to Chris' full on riding style, and after a meeting with Brian Martin it looked like he'd landed works bikes for '65, although as he told me it didn't quite turn out as planned.

"Brian Martin offered me a brace of works (250 & 500) BSAs for the 1965 season, but a week before I was due to pick the bikes up pulled out of the deal."

The 'official' reason given for this change of plan was that "Matchless and BSA had an agreement not to sign each others riders." However, the feeling with those in the know was that one of BSA's top riders viewed Horsfield as a serious threat to his own championship aspirations and simply didn't want him in the same team, therefore vetoing his ride.

Despite his superlative riding skills Chris had been struggling to get the best out of the heavy Matchless, so unbeknown to his bosses at AMC he set about improving the handling with a visit to the Rickman brothers.

"Derek Rickman had already shown that with a decent frame the Matchless could still be competitive, so I got Bob Cooper to prepare it and fabricate some titanium engine plates ready to slot the works engine straight in without interrupting my racing schedule. As you can imagine it was a revelation after the works heavyweight, and weighed in at 278lb – a huge saving over the works bike."

It was aboard this Metisse-framed bike I first saw Chris in action at a bitterly cold BBC Grandstand trophy scramble at Naish Hill near Lacock, in the winter of 1965. In the same year AMC itself had also announced a 'new' machine, which if nothing else certainly looked purposeful; sadly, as Chris revealed, the design, testing and costing of the new scrambler left a lot to be desired.

"The frame had been designed around a chalk outline drawn on the floor at Woolwich, and although it looked fantastic it didn't handle at all well and Vic Eastwood's father immediately went about cutting and modifying the rear end and steering head angle. It was wheeled out for the attendant press pack who made all the right sort of noises, but when questioned how much it was going to cost Bill Smith passed it on to Ernie who replied 'got to be worth £279 of anybody's money.' I got the impression that up to that point there had been little or no thought given to the cost and it was figure which was just plucked out of the air!"

There was no doubt that Chris was one of the best 500cc riders of his era, a talent not unnoticed in the Eastern bloc and one of its star riders Joel Robert. His tip off regarding AMC's imminent collapse of course soon came to fruition, but by then Horsfield was on his way to CZ and a works ride on the Czechoslovakian 2-strokes.

"At that time I was racing most of the year in Belgium and based in Brussels, where I'd become good friends with Joel Robert and Roger De Coster. I'd met Robert when he first came to England as an up and coming eighteen year old, and even then you could see he was an incredibly talented rider and a champion in the making.

I'd given my bikes back to Matchless so he (Joel) suggested I went with him to the works at Strakonice to try for a factory CZ. I tested the bikes and then had to go before a committee of twelve including the

Chris leading the inter-centre team scramble in 1964.

Topping up the Matchless' oil at Minety Vale in August 1964.

Off-Road Giants!

'main man' Mr Jarrolim. Despite having the gears on the 'wrong side' the bikes were fantastic with broad spread of power, and compared to the old Matchless, so light that they felt more like a high speed push bike. Jarrolim – who always took pride in being called Mister – knew all about my successes in the TV trophy and immediately offered me two bikes, a 250 and 500, plus a mechanic and spares for the rest of the series.

They duly arrived in the UK, although the first time I saw or sat on them was before practice at the TV scramble at Builth Wells; I took to them immediately and managed to finish second in both the 250 and 500cc races."

On the potent twin port 360cc CZ Chris was capable of taking on and beating almost anyone, and the name of Horsfield was being touted as a possible World championship contender. As history would record, there were numerous other TV trophy and British championship wins, but in the GPs that all important consistency and reliability just eluded him. Smith had retained his crown in '65, but in 1966 the CZ-mounted quartet of Friedrichs, Tiblin, Horsfield and Bickers were a season long thorn in the BSA man's side. Smith was very quick and perhaps unlucky not to make it a hat trick, but after a long hard season East German Friedrichs eventually took the title, although Chris, as he told me, was left very frustrated.

"The 360cc CZ was a fantastic machine to ride, but in those days the GP was decided over two legs, and there were numerous times where after doing well in leg one I would be sidelined in the second by some niggling breakdown. By the end of the season – in which I managed to finish fourth – we'd also run out of spares; incidentally, it was written into my contract that if I finished in the championship top five I was allowed to keep my bike."

Travelling the length and breadth of Europe saw Chris put thousands of miles on his race transport, and he recalled that in his quest for title honours in '66 he did 85,000 in his Zodiac car and trailer.

The GPs took him to some very unusual and inhospitable places, none more so than the barren steppes of the Soviet Union.

"It was the height of the Cold War so the Soviets were very uneasy about letting Westerners in, and they certainly didn't want us travelling around without an official escort. They'd arranged for us to drive in convoy with 'minders' in their painfully slow old Ladas. The flat landscape just seemed to go on forever, and after a while we couldn't stand the frustration of travelling at 30mph any longer so Rolf Tiblin shouted 'let's go' and we disappeared in a cloud of dust. It started to get dark and miles away across the steppes we could see the twinkling of lights; as we got closer we could see it was a huge caravan of gipsies pulled up for the night so we asked if the four of us, Rolf, Jerry, Per-Olaf Perrson and me could join them. It was probably the first time they had seen Westerners but they were wonderful hosts; they treated us to singing and dancing around the campfires and after we'd eaten the specially prepared goat's meat we slept under the stars. Needless to say, when our minders eventually caught up the following day they were not very pleased!"

Fourth in 1966 would prove to be Horsfield's high spot in the world championship standings, although as he demonstrated his career still had plenty of mileage in it. After an indifferent season on the CZ in '67 Chris was lured away to Thundersley and a works contract with Greeves, but things didn't quite work out how he'd hoped. Eric Cheney had seen that the days of the 'big bangers' were numbered and had fitted a Greeves Challenger motor into one of his exquisitely crafted frames, the 250cc version of which was tested in the December '66 *Motor Cycle* by staffer Peter Fraser. He came away highly impressed by the sure handling 2-stroke, his report concluding with the words 'a top flight rider in either 250 or 360 form will have the championship loaded in his favour.' That rider should have been Chris, but it didn't happen.

"It was potentially a very good machine and featured fully floating brakes and carried the fuel under the seat. This left the 'tank' as merely a shroud for the up and over exhaust system and the HT coil. After commissioning Eric to make it, Bert Greeves wouldn't allow me to ride it because he wanted to stick with the aluminium beam frame."

As the history books record, little more than a year later Greeves would eventually replace the H-piece frame with its new Griffon, so it was a frustrated Horsfield who campaigned the '67 season on a pair of 250/360 works prepared Challengers. Nevertheless he had some good rides and recorded both British championship and TV trophy wins at Lancashire's Cuerdon Park and Hawkstone. This was all before a heavy crash and resultant broken neck bone brought both his season and association with Greeves to a premature end.

Not only was Chris a top line rider, he'd learnt a lot about machine setup and preparation, skills which were soon being sought by a new kid on the block, Kawasaki. Although as he soon found out, the Japanese firm had a lot to learn about the requirements of a motocross bike.

"Motocross was starting to really take off, especially in America, and Kawasaki – understandably keen to be part of this potentially huge market – asked me to ride and help develop its bike. It was a rotary valve 2-stroke but the power delivery and handling was all wrong. It needed totally redesigning to make it competitive and I started to look around for other rides."

History would record that barely a decade later a Kawasaki ridden by Brad Lackey would scoop the world championship, but for Chris it was time to move to a prime job with AJS. Following the collapse of AMC, the company and its famous names of James, Norton and AJS had been taken over by Manganese Bronze and re-emerged under the umbrella of Norton Villiers. For Chris it was a case of full circle, as the machine he was asked to ride and develop was the AJS Stormer, a machine powered by virtually the same engine he had worked on during his days at Wolverhampton.

"Although the James didn't handle particularly well the engine showed a lot of potential, but development was always held back by lack of money. Norton Villiers was keen to have a motocross bike in its range and allocated a budget of £87,000 to develop the Stormer, this under the team led by Peter Inchley and Fluff Brown."

In Malcolm Davis and Andy Roberton AJS had already recruited two top class riders, and it came as little or no surprise when in '68 Davis won the 250cc British championship. A year later a 370 version appeared, and in addition to Chris a plethora of top class riders, including ex-AMC team-mate Vic Eastwood, Roger Harvey, Rob Hooper, Dick Clayton and Arthur Browning all notched up memorable victories on the sure footed 2-strokes.

Throughout his long career he was always on the lookout for new rides and new challenges, and the following season saw a 4-stroke-mounted Horsfield come to the start gate. The fans loved the sound of the booming 'big bangers' and the Rickmans – who had long campaigned for a big 4-stroke class – were quick to sign him when the new 750cc European championship was announced. Chris – who was the first 'official works Rickman rider' – lined up on the potent mark four Metisse, although as he told me it proved to be a rather 'up and down' season.

"The engine was a full blown 500cc BSA fitted with a Weslake four valve head. It went like the clappers and after the first couple of rounds I was leading the championship. However, it only needed the zener diode to smell water and it would stop dead, an ongoing problem which eventually scuppered my chances."

Sadly, the new championship which started with high hopes ended the year in confusion; one round was inexplicably cancelled and in Switzerland lap scoring and rider identification became impossible when the course turned into a mud bath. It was some time later that the FIM announced that Derek Rickman was the first (and only) European 750cc champion, with fellow team member Horsfield runner-up. Not only did Chris ride the BSA Metisse, he also rode a Rickman-supplied Bultaco on the near continent, although by 1970 he was on his way stateside to some lucrative earnings.

"Motocross was taking off in America so Husky importer and enterprising promoter Edison Dye arranged for a group of us including Dave Bickers, John Banks, Robert, De Coster, Mikola and myself to take on the Yanks. It was a high profile series attracting the best of the American riders, including Steve McQueen and Bud Ekins. It generated some good earnings too; CZ paid me £2000 before I went, and on top of that I also retained all of my prize money – good pay for 1970."

Riding a CZ supplied by the American importer Chris went back to the States for three more seasons, but following a nasty crash he returned home in '72, heavily plastered and considering his future.

"It had been a horrific crash and one I was lucky to escape from without really serious injury, so I considered calling it a day. Well I did but decided I was going to race 'one last time' at a meeting near Lyon; a race for which the organisers presented the winner with a gold bar worth about £800. I'd already won it twice and thought it would be good to retire on a high with victory number three. Sadly, it was not to be because I crashed again, so my career ended up not on the rostrum but in the medics tent."

Rather ironic, perhaps, that Chris' long and highly successful career which started with a crash through a hedge in Warwickshire should also end in the same way in France.

For twelve eventful years he'd followed his dream of being a professional scrambler, and became arguably one of the best riders of his generation – and who knows, with a bit more luck in '66 he could have been best in the world.

Chris leading Jeff Smith at the 1965 Hants Grand National.

Dave at an Enborne scramble – AMC used this photo in much of its period advertising.

Scrambling in the 1950s was the domain of strong men, with not only riding ability but also the strength to bend the grudging bikes to their will. Dave Curtis was one of the best.

CHAPTER 7
DAVE CURTIS

It's the Brill scramble course in the summer of 1948. Racing is over for the day, and as the dust settles, spectators and competitors pack up and head for home, among them a farmer's young son who's made his scrambles debut on an old twin port, girder-forked Ariel; a bike which he had ridden eight miles to the event and then raced over the rough demanding circuit. As he kicked the Ariel back into shape little could he have imagined that, ten years later, not only would he be a works Matchless rider, but also an integral member of the Motocross Des Nations team, and that D G Curtis would be wearing the crown of British 500cc motocross champion. Tenacious and strong as an ox – ideal attributes to control 380lb of booming Matchless – the hard riding man from Oxfordshire was one of the most popular riders of his generation, and for me – an unashamed Curtis fan – it was a great privilege to meet him and talk about his long career.

If the course was rough or muddy then you could usually bet that Dave Curtis would be out in front, and numerous period photographs show him sliding the monstrous AMC single with the pack in distant pursuit. So how did he become such a 'master of the mud,' I asked him?

"My dad rode a bit, and even from an early age there was a bike around on the farm on which my brothers Mike and Roger and I learnt to ride. It was a flat tank Raleigh which we used for tearing around the fields after school, and I got pretty good at negotiating the deep ruts and mud left by the wheels of the tractors and the cows. The farm was very remote so all three of us would get on the bike and ride it the two miles to the nearest village; this was a bit precarious, especially in winter. One would drive while another was perched on the pillion pad, leaving the third to straddle the petrol tank and hold a torch to show the way. I really fancied a go at scrambling, so as soon as I was old enough I managed to borrow a girder-forked Ariel from my cousin and entered a meeting at nearby Brill, a fantastic but very rough and muddy course lined by thousands of people. I can't actually remember much about the race but I loved the whole excitement and atmosphere so I decided to get my own bike."

As for many of his contemporaries there was no possibility of a specialised 'scrambler,' so a road going 500cc Matchless was pressed into action, a bike on which the young Curtis soon displayed his potential.

"After a while I managed to get upgraded to Expert status and notched up my first win. The bike had quite a hard life as there was no

48

Early outings at the March Hare scramble in 1958.

At the national Wessex scramble at Glastonbury in 1960.

Off-Road Giants!

way I could afford a car or pick-up, so it had to be ridden to the events where we would take off the number plates, lights and silencer, and after the day's racing replace them and ride home."

For all of his undoubted raw talent it was obvious that to progress further a more competitive machine was needed, and thanks to his father, Dave lined up for the '52 season aboard a brace of BSAs.

"Dad bought me a 500cc BSA which featured a high lift cam engine and a McCandless rear swinging arm. The engine ran on dope which made it very quick, but I was plagued by bent pushrods. It thrived on plenty of revs but on one occasion my race was brought to an early end when the barrel blew clean off the crankcases."

As with many farmers Curtis Senior was a master at 'make and mend' and later fabricated his own rear swinging arm to a second BSA, a bike on which as Dave told me earned his first works ride, with Ariel.

"I was aware that some of the factories were keeping an eye on me, although it was a pleasant surprise when Ariel's competition chief Clive Bennett asked me if I would like to try one of the works 500s. It was a good bike, and in one of my three races I managed to bring it home third in the Lanc's Grand National. This was before I got a request from AMC competition boss Hugh Viney asking if 'I would like to go and see them?' I went along and they offered me a pair – 350 and 500cc – of works prepared singles."

As can be appreciated it didn't take Dave very long to agree, whereupon he was introduced to Jock West for what would be the start of a long and successful association between the rider and AMC. This would last for the next nine years – an association which brought Curtis fame and acclaim, but as he told me little in the way of financial rewards from the factory.

"I was introduced to Jock West who shook my hand – commenting on how strong my grip was – followed by the words 'for the love of the sport'. I rode Matchless for the rest of my career but from that day onward never received a penny in retainer or financial reward from the company."

AMC might have been rather tight fisted about paying one of their star riders, but with top quality machines and the status befitting a works man Dave was able to pick up decent prize and start money, especially from the lucrative continental meetings.

"Les Archer had quickly cottoned on that there was good money to be earned racing in France, and became very good at not only sourcing the best events but also negotiating the most lucrative rates of pay, all of these negotiations helped immensely by Les' wife, who was French."

Dave had now progressed to a Standard pick-up to transport the bikes, and he recalled that for his first trip to the continent he – plus pick-up and bikes – flew on the Silver City service from Lydd to Le Touquet. Not surprisingly he soon established himself as a favourite with the continental crowds, although as he told me he owed much to the enthusiasm of his boss for these regular trips to Europe.

"My dad had been initially a tenant farmer, and then became farm manager for the Baronet Sir Algernon Peyton – he also owned the entire local village and most of the land around – so when my father died at the young age of 58 the Baronet invited me to take over managing the farm. This could have put the kibosh on my scrambling but Sir Algernon was a real gentleman, he wasn't out to make loads of money and as long as things ticked over quietly he was more than happy. In fact he actively encouraged me to race abroad and I recall that one year I went to the continent over twenty times."

Many of these trips were made with the likes of Les Archer, John Draper and Jeff Smith, 'opposition' works riders and fierce rivals on the track but good friends off. A typical weekend would involve travelling on the Friday, practising on the Saturday, and returning home after the race on Sunday for work on Monday morning. All this travelling obviously put a lot of miles on a vehicle resulting in the inevitable breakdown, which sometimes called for a bit of lateral thinking and improvisation.

"I'd progressed to a car and trailer and we were on our way to a meeting when we suddenly 'lost' the trailer. Fortunately I managed to stop and discovered that the draw bar had snapped. We were in the middle of nowhere so there was no other alternative than to get some stakes from a field and make a splint held together by barbed wire, remarkably it all held together until we could get it welded up."

There was none prouder to represent his country than D G Curtis and his debut ride came in the 1954 Motocross Des Nations at Pay-Bas in Holland. Dave was a member of the victorious team comprising himself, Geoff Ward (AJS) and Brian Stonebridge (Matchless). For the next seven years he would be a regular member of the British line-up which would also celebrate victory in 1957 (Smith, Martin, Curtis) and 1960 with Jeff Smith and Don Rickman. 1954 was a memorable year for Curtis and one in which he announced himself as a man capable of taking on and beating the best in the world. The British round of the European championships that year was held at Hawkstone Park, a demanding 1½ mile circuit that, amongst other hazards, featured a 70mph straight and a daunting hill – a track ideally suited to Dave's hard riding style. Scrambles had huge spectator appeal, and by the time the tickets ran out, over 33,000 people had paid their 3/6d to watch the 15 lap main event. It turned into a race of attrition as first early leader Geoff Ward crashed out and then Auguste Mingels FN suffered carburation problems. 1952 and '53 British GP winner Brian Stonebridge led for a while before he injured a thumb, and just before the end Bill Nilsson also crashed. When the flag fell Phil Nex took victory, closely followed by Curtis, David Tye, Les Archer and Terry Cheshire for an all British top five. The crowd went wild with excitement.

Riding these huge 4-strokes called for a special breed of rider, and Dave – who thanks to his work on the farm had built up a lot of upper body strength – told me a little about that 1954 season and what it was like to ride the works Matchless.

"It was a great honour to be selected for the Motocross Des Nations and wonderful to be on the winning team, but my lasting memory is the photograph which appeared the following week – this showed Geoff, Brian and I looking absolutely shattered after our endeavours. The bike was very fast but it weighed the best part of 380lb, and with only three inches of suspension movement at the back and about four at the front it gave your body a hell of a pounding."

There was little doubt that the works bikes would have benefited greatly from lighter frames – the roadster-based clamped-up swinging arm was prone to twisting – and better suspension. Sadly, requests to the comp department usually fell on deaf ears and it was left to the riders to implement improvements.

"It was AMC's policy that 'you rode what they gave you', and there was a considerable amount of controversy when we discarded the jampots and replaced them with the lighter and superior Girling

"WITH ONLY THREE INCHES OF SUSPENSION MOVEMENT AT THE BACK AND ABOUT FOUR AT THE FRONT IT GAVE YOUR BODY A HELL OF A POUNDING"

Dave leads Don Rickman – unusually wearing no 75 – at the Berkshire GN in 1960.

Off-Road Giants!

units. After a while even the factory could see that the bikes handled much better with the Girlings, so it begrudgingly allowed us to race with them, but insisted that when they went back to the comp shop for fettling we put the jampots back on! We were left pretty much to our own devices as to what events we entered, but the factory stipulated that we had to attend all of the trade-supported nationals. Doing well in these was good advertising material for the company, and for a win or decent position I would pick up an extra £5 or so from the likes of Dunlop, Castrol and KLG spark plugs. Incidentally, although the bike went back to the factory on a regular basis, between races the riders were expected to carry out all of their own maintenance work."

Dave loved racing on the continent where there were often points to be won in pursuit of the European, and later the world championships. Indeed, with a bit of luck he could have been crowned best in the world, as in 1959 he was leading the championship up until the Danish round when cruelly the Matchless' chain snapped, handing the title to his great rival Swede Sten Lundin ahead of Bill Nilsson, with Curtis a close third.

If there was a best-ever season for D G Curtis then it has to be 1958, a year in which Dave was almost unbeatable in the UK and one in which he ran out comfortable 500cc British championship winner. There were numerous wins on both the 350 and 500cc machines and also on a big bore 600, which he rode to victory in both the Cotswold and Experts Grand Nationals, events where the regulations didn't specify a maximum of 500cc. In the glutinous Cotswold mud Curtis and the big banger were a formidable and – for five years on the trot – unrivalled combination in the Gloucestershire classic.

Following stateside requests for the G80 CS to have more cubes, Dave had been asked by AMC to evaluate the 600cc motor. Fed by a huge GP5 carb, the engine – which turned out 46bhp – never went into production, although it was later used in the Matchless Metisse which Derek Rickman rode to victory in the 1966 750cc European championships.

Not only was 1958 a successful year for Curtis in the UK, he also notched up international motocross wins in Austria, France and Sweden and followed up his ISDT gold of '56 with another at Garmisch Partenkirchen in Germany. Riding for the British Trophy team in what many observers regarded as one of the easiest trials since the war, Dave was one of 109 from the 246 starters who won gold, although as he told me the six days wasn't his favourite event.

"AMC had a long history of competing in the ISDT, and I was asked if I would represent the British Vase B team comprising David Tye, Sid Wicken, Ken Heanes and myself for the 1956 event, which incidentally was also based at Garmisch. Prior to the 'six dayer' we were entered in a three day trial in Austria to get a feel for what these long distance events were all about. We arrived at the start to find that the first 'day' was in fact a night run; clearly this information hadn't got through to AMC because although we had a battery none of our bikes were fitted with a generator, so we set off knowing that we would soon have no lights. All three of us on Matchless tagged on to a German rider who was going particularly well and stuck to his rear lamp like limpets. We were so close we knocked him off once, but eventually I got detached and lost my way in the forest. There was a terrific thunderstorm going on and the only illumination I had was from the lightning flashing overhead. The water was rushing down the tracks like a river and I eventually found my way to a village and a checkpoint. I got some very strange looks because I'd arrived from the 'wrong way', but with no lights I had no other alternative than to retire."

In the ISDT event itself the British quartet arrived at the last day speed test along with Holland B, Germany A and Poland A all on gold medal schedule, but they knew that the odds were stacked against them in favour of the smaller capacity machines. Curtis' 500cc Matchless was actually passed by Westphal's 250cc NSU at over 90mph, but all hope of team glory was gone when Dave Tye lost his Ariels dynamo and along with it his own gold medal.

"To be honest I got an incredibly sore backside from sitting on the bike all day for six days, and in truth found the ISDT to be rather boring. I was asked to ride again but declined, so 1958 was my second and last year."

The many trips to mainland Europe left Dave with scores of happy memories, although as he told me one to north Africa left him fearing for his safety and well being.

"AMC had a dealership in Algiers, and it was arranged that Geoff Ward and I fly out to take part in the race and provide a bit of publicity for the importer. The race was held in what looked like a quarry and on arrival we found it a bit disconcerting to see armed guards standing around the perimeter fence. It got under way and Geoff and I were soon dicing for the lead with a Frenchman – at that time Algeria was under French control – who was obviously a favourite with the crowd, and they went absolutely crazy when there was a collision involving 'their rider,' Geoff and myself and he crashed out. They were screaming for our blood and at the end of the race we had to be smuggled out under cover in the back of a car. Just to cap it all, Geoff had (against good advice) drunk some of the local water and was extremely ill for the return flight home."

Dave didn't much take to the smooth, fast southern circuits but at Hawkstone he was in his element, and vividly recalled the day in 1960 when over fifty thousand (75,000 according to the *Daily Herald*) turned up to pay respect to the late Brian Stonebridge. Over the years the Matchless had received little in the way of improvements, but Curtis was still a formidable rider, and to remind everyone he was still one of the best riders in the world he won both races at the British motocross GP the following year. TV brought scrambles and the names of its star riders into thousands of homes and in the wintry, often muddy conditions the tenacious man from Oxfordshire was usually seen fighting for the lead. A legacy of those days for a lad from Somerset (yours truly) is a now long faded photograph of D G Curtis broadsiding the Matchless through the Carleon mud in 1963. I mentioned this to Dave and he laughed and said:

"I think I fell off just after that photo was taken! At the end of '62 I decided to retire and handed the bikes back to the factory, but I couldn't stay away and a year later bought myself a Matchless Metisse to 'ride and enjoy' in the 63/64 winter TV season. Of course everyone still expected me to be winning, but I was up against 'youngsters' like Chris Horsfield who had taken over my former works bike, so at the end of that season I finally called it a day."

His modest nature and never-say-die style undoubtedly made Dave Curtis one of the most popular and successful riders of his time, and it was great pleasure to talk to him about those joyous days of scrambling.

At the start of the 1963 Cotswold scramble.

"HIS MODEST NATURE AND NEVER-SAY-DIE STYLE UNDOUBTEDLY MADE DAVE CURTIS ONE OF THE MOST POPULAR AND SUCCESSFUL RIDERS OF HIS TIME"

At the Hants GN in 1964 – not Dave's favourite circuit.

Fluff on the 250cc Cotton at the BBC TV scramble at Clifton. (Photo Morton's archive)

From a beginning as a keen amateur scrambler to televised off-road success, to sought-after development engineer and then manufacturer, Fluff Brown has enjoyed a long and varied career and is still actively involved to this day.

CHAPTER 8
FLUFF BROWN - AJS & COTTON

Like many aspiring off-road stars, Fluff Brown's scrambles debut in the season of 1952 was a fairly modest affair. Along with many of his contemporaries a specialist competition machine was out of the question, so his ride to work 197cc Ambassador was pressed into the dual role of day to day 'hack' and weekend scrambles iron. Getting the bike to the event was in itself quite an adventure, as there was no added luxury of a tow car and trailer or pick-up. Instead, with a knobbly tyre strapped across his shoulder, the little 2-stroke was ridden to the meetings where, after being stripped of superfluous items like lights and silencer and a change of rubber, it was ready for a day of thrills and the inevitable spills. And with racing over for the day, it was kicked back into shape and re-equipped for the homeward return, a hard introduction to the world of scrambling for the young Brown.

Fluff didn't set the world on fire in that first season but it started him on the road to a long and illustrious scrambles career; little then could he have imagined that by the following decade he would be a works Cotton rider and – courtesy of Saturday afternoon TV scrambles – a household name. Not only did Fluff prove to be a top class rider and development engineer, he later also displayed a keen eye for business – on the collapse of NVT in 1974 he bought all of the stock for the AJS Stormer motocrosser and with it the manufacturing rights to the illustrious name. For the last thirty years Fluff, along with son Nick and their staff have continued to keep the name of both AJS and Cotton alive on the world's classic motocross scene, so to find out more about both him and the business today I journeyed to their base in rural Hampshire.

As it transpired it was a good time to visit, as Nick had exciting news concerning the first road bike to wear the AJS logo in over forty years, but we'll return to that later. I started by asking Brown Senior how his riding and racing careers started and how he came to be called Fluff?

"I was born in Chillington, which is a little village in Somerset. During my early days a school chum by the name of Eddie Bussell started calling me Fluff and it's stuck ever since – everybody including my bank manager now knows me by it. Most people wouldn't have a clue what my real name is. My dad owned a 250cc Triumph which he taught me to ride before I was legally old enough, but Chillington was a quiet village and you could go up and down virtually all day without seeing another vehicle. I became interested in scrambling through a local chap called Wally 'Manka' Matthews. Wally was quite a good

54

Fluff just managing to keep ahead of Don Rickman's Bultaco Metisse.

Practising with team-mate Jim Timms on their 360cc Cottons. (Photo Morton's archive)

Off-Road Giants!

rider in the Wessex centre and in the evenings after school he would allow me to ride his scrambler around the fields. After sampling Wally's bike I desperately wanted to go racing, but of course in those days there were no schoolboy events so I had to wait until I was sixteen. I loved tearing across the fields and as soon as I was old enough bought an Ambassador to ride to work on. On my apprentice wages I couldn't afford to buy another bike so there was no other option than to scramble the road bike. I can't remember much about the first event other than I fell off quite a few times which left me rather bruised and the bike out of shape."

For the next two years under Wally's guidance Fluff continued to race and improve, until like most young men of his generation he was called up for two years national service. Scrambling was put on hold, although as he explained it didn't curtail or hinder his motorcycling exploits.

"I was conscripted into the Royal Engineers training regiment for despatch riders and served my time with several other keen motorcyclists including Ken Heanes, who later became such a great ISDT star. Our bikes were standard issue BSA side valve M20/M21s which not surprisingly we got to know inside out. They also provided us with a lot of fun, as after the 'big wigs' has departed on a Saturday afternoon we rode them around the parade ground stood on the seat with our arms crossed."

This balancing skill obviously stood Fluff in good stead because with army service done it was back to civvy street and a return to scrambles aboard a 197cc Sun, which was soon replaced by a similar capacity Dot. In the 1950s 2-stroke tuning was still very much a dark art, and in an effort to keep up with the opposition Fluff wrote to Dot for some tips on how to make his bike faster; the reply, however, was not what he was expecting.

"The factory Dots really flew, and in open unlimited capacity races regularly managed to beat machines twice their engine size. I thought that I might get some tuning tips so I wrote a letter, but the reply was disappointing as the only advice I received was to buy a new set of piston rings!"

Throughout his career Fluff's build was ideally suited to lightweight 2-strokes, and his solitary outing on a big banger left him reeling.

"My cousin was racing a 500cc BSA Gold Star scrambler and asked me if I fancied trying it. It weighed in at around 350lb and felt huge after the Dot. The vibration was horrendous and by the end of the race it felt like my eyes were going around like marbles in a jam jar!"

While the Goldie might have been Fluff's first and last race on a 500, by 1956 he'd achieved Expert status and bought his first Cotton – but it was not just his riding skills that were getting noticed.

He was becoming adept and skilled with the workings of the Villiers scrambles motor, and was approached to fettle the Cotton ridden by Badger Goss. Badger's success on the Brown-prepared bikes made Cotton's principal duo of Pat Onions and Monty Denly sit up and take notice – "I want that man up here," said Denly, and it wasn't long before he was on his way to Gloucester. He was taken on in the dual role of rider and development engineer, and it heralded the start of a long, happy and successful association between Fluff and the Cotton factory. Incidentally, this was also Nick Brown's first introduction to motorcycling as at one month old he was pictured with his father sat on the works bike. On both the scrambles circuits and in the development shop the combination of Fluff and Cotton became a winning formula, although it was as Brown the racer he perhaps became best known. At virtually any open to centre or national lightweight race in the early sixties his tenacious but smooth riding style would usually see him battling for the lead, something I first witnessed at a bitterly cold and muddy TV scramble at Naish Hill in 1962. With the luxury afforded to a works man Fluff had long since progressed to a tow car and trailer to transport the bikes, but after an incident returning from a wintry Beaulieu some lateral thinking was called for, as he explained.

"I think it was about 1963 and along with my friend and fellow Cotton rider Jim Timms we towed the bikes to a very snowy Beaulieu TV scramble behind my Hillman Minx. It was extremely difficult racing on the hard packed snow and we all slipped and slithered a lot, which probably made a great spectacle for the armchair fans. On the way back home we had an accident, and although both of us and the car were undamaged the trailer was written off and one of the bikes left bent and buckled. This left us in a dilemma as were due to ride in an event at Accrington the following day, so we partially stripped the bikes and managed to squeeze both of them into the boot of the Hillman. It wasn't an easy drive but we eventually got back to Gloucester where we transferred the one useable bike into the back of a borrowed Landrover and set off north. It was a freezing cold night and the heater didn't work but we eventually arrived about six o'clock the following morning. We knocked up the organiser whose wife took pity on us and cooked up a wonderful fried breakfast. We only had the one bike which we had to share, but fortunately we didn't both get into the same final."

Like many small manufacturers Cotton's continually walked a financial tightrope, but despite this it managed to attract some top names and was involved with some interesting development work. So, what was it like to be involved in development at that time?

"A lot of well known names joined the Cotton fold including scramblers Ken Messenger, John Draper, Freddie Mayes, the Lampkin brothers, Malcolm Davis, and Bill Ivey on the Telstar road-racer. We did a lot of engine development work with Cross Manufacturing in Bath and also with Peter Inchley at Villiers on the prototype Starmaker motor."

Much of the static development of the engines was carried out on the test bed in Fluff's galvanised workshop, although in the days prior to health and safety legislation no one considered the effect this might have. Tests frequently involved running the open megaphone engines up to speed, and on one occasion Fluff had to be picked up off the floor after becoming dizzy and collapsing with the noise. Fitted with two massive Amal GP carbs, the Starmaker engine was turning out a heady 25bhp at 6000rpm, but this quickly showed up the limitations in the lightweight Cotton frame and breakages were frequent. This was eventually cured when the factory adopted an oval top tube to the headstock.

Much of the track tests and chassis developments took place at Hawkstone Park, although a typical day, which involved a detour to the Villiers factory at Wolverhampton, was often a long and frustrating one, especially when blighted by a broken frame.

Fluff continued to successfully race in both the UK and the near continent, but development wasn't just limited to the use of the Villiers engine. Given the success achieved by the Rickman brothers on their Triumph powered Metisse, the unit twin seemed to be an obvious choice of motive power. A young Andy Roberton joined the team, and by 1965

Fluff with the brand-new 360cc Cotton.
(Photo Morton's archive)

With Cotton team-mates Joe Johnson and Jim Timms.

Off-Road Giants!

frame kits to accommodate the Triumph engine were available at £109. Like most other small manufacturers Cotton was by then exploiting the British purchase tax rules which stated that a machine sold in kit form was exempt from paying tax, and therefore it sold considerably cheaper than a ready to race machine.

Fluff was fully involved in this project which would feature again later on in his career, but after seven years at Gloucester his development skills were being sought elsewhere.

His work with Peter Inchley and Dr Baur had not gone unnoticed, and when Villiers came under the umbrella of the newly formed Norton/Villiers he was invited to join the team. Fluff takes up the story again:

"The Starmaker engine had proven its potential, but up until then it had appeared only in other manufacturer's frames so a new rolling chassis was required. Initially we housed it in a Petite Metisse frame and Freddie Mayes raced it in both the 1966 British championship and selected GPs as a Villiers Metisse. Andy Roberton couldn't get on with the Metisse frame so we modified a Cotton one which he took to like a duck to water."

This frame would be the one which later appeared in the production bike carrying the name of AJS Stormer.

"At this time I was still working in Gloucester, and every morning at 6.00am would pick up Andy for the long commute to the Villiers works in Wolverhampton. The Stormer was launched in a blaze of publicity and included some with an up-and-coming road-racer called Barry Sheene. I think he got paid about £25 and had his lunch provided for being photographed on the bike – a couple of years later when he became famous he was probably being paid thousands to open a supermarket! With a decent frame and forks the Stormer proved to be a very competitive bike, and in 1967 Malcolm Davis won the British championship on one; not only did we make the 250 but also a 370, which eventually got stretched to 410cc. In addition to Malcolm we managed to attract some other top class riders to the team including Vic Eastwood, Chris Horsfield, Roger Harvey, Rob Hooper, Dick Clayton, and that great all-rounder Arthur Browning. Arthur wasn't one of our regular riders, but I recall that we let him borrow a 410 which he took to Cadwell Park and promptly won the Grandstand trophy on. In 1970 the production of the Stormer had been transferred to Andover, but to begin with I was still travelling from Gloucester each and every day. By this time I'd taken on a variety of job roles, including that of competition manager and 'dealer liaison person'– this covered a multitude of things from discussing technical matters to chasing up unpaid debts."

By the early seventies NVT was on the slide, and when closure came in 1974 Fluff was quick to see that the Stormer still had some life left in it, as he told me.

"Many of the dealers were encouraging me to continue production, so I put in a sensible offer to buy all of the stock. This was accepted and we moved to Flint's farm near Andover in September 1974. By then I'd moved from Gloucester, so not only was the site at Goodworth Clatford handy to where I lived, it had the added bonus of carrying low overheads. I was joined by Reg Painter who had also worked for Norton's, and basically we just carried on what we enjoyed doing, making and selling motorbikes. The stock comprised a lot of complete 410cc engines, so we set up a little production line making four bikes at a time."

Although the Spanish and Japanese machines were carrying all before them on the national and GP circuits, the Stormer was still a good clubman's bike and the engine also found its way into several other uses. Legendary MCC trials exponent Jack Pouncey used one to power his long distance trials outfit, and two specials were made for the Wiltshire constabulary. These were made so the police could train for 'off road' duties on the nearby Salisbury plain, but if Fluff is to be believed they (the bikes, not the bobbies) were lost in a bottomless bog and never seen again. Much of the work on the police bikes had been carried out by Fluff's son Nick, who after serving an apprenticeship at Boscombe Down worked as both a precision engineer and in the vehicle repair business, before joining his father in 1989.

Not only have the Browns kept the name of AJS alive, there are few classic and pre-'65 scrambles where the Cotton's ridden by Gary Wilkinson and the evergreen Andy Roberton don't feature in the results. Something which as Nick explained came almost about by accident.

"We were approached by one of our Stormer owners, David Heaton, to build him a Cotton to race in pre-'65 scrambles. Classic and pre-'65 scrambling was by then just starting to get popular, so we needed to make sure that the frame was as accurate to the period as possible. We borrowed a frame from Ally Clift and made what we thought would perhaps be a one-off, but soon had requests from not only the UK but also from as far away as Sweden from people who wanted replicas. In total we've made about sixty five complete bikes and frame kits including the 250MX Starmaker and 500cc Triumph powered motocrosser, a 250 Telstar roadracer and also a 250 trials bike with a Starmaker engine."

Nick didn't achieve the same riding heights as his father, but at a time when almost everyone else was mounted on a Maico he successfully campaigned a Stormer against the best in the local AMCA clubs, Alton and Andover. It was at one of these meetings in 1993 that they first saw Gary Wilkinson. Mounted on a 250 Stormer, Gary's forceful riding style stood out from the rest and soon he was mounted on one of the Browns specially prepared Cotton's, a machine which over the years he's notched up numerous wins on. The other part of the 'works duo' is Andy Roberton, a man who's ridden Cottons for much of his career and was barely out of boyhood when Fluff first met him in the 1960s – indeed, Andy can remember a time when he used to babysit for the young Nick!

Remember when Fluff took over the production of the Stormer in 1974 there was no such thing as classic racing, but with the upsurge of interest in bikes from that era the single cylinder AJS continues to be a competitive and reliable mount.

"I was someone who happened to be in the right place at the right time," he told me, "and the continued production has certainly been a true labour of love. We have a steady turnover in parts which are sent as far afield as New Zealand and the United States, and we take pride that we have 100 per cent spares availability. Some of these like exhaust systems are made in-house, while other castings are farmed out to suppliers both at home and overseas."

During my visit Fluff had two machines in his workshop which were undergoing refurbishment, but as I previously mentioned this is not the only side to the business or the end of the AJS story. For the last six or seven years Nick has concentrated his efforts on setting up and expanding on the company's working relationship with a major manufacturer in China; a potentially exciting project.

"I became increasingly aware of the burgeoning capabilities of the Chinese after a visit to the NEC show during the late 1990s. I saw

FLUFF BROWN - AJS & COTTON

their version of a Honda monkey bike and came back home with a handful of leaflets, although I must admit that at the time I felt a bit like the boy who went out with a cow and came back home with a handful of beans. I got very interested in the possibility of importing some of their bikes, so we went out on a fact-finding trip. This was not without its problems as there are scores of manufacturers and suppliers in every city, but after a lot of time and research we signed a contract with Jianshe in 1999 which, due to its tie-up with Yamaha, is one of the best in regards to Western market quality requirements."

Tales about dealing with Chinese red tape and bureaucracy and setting up an agent is something for another book, but Nick then went on to tell me how things had developed.

"With the deal signed we acquired a warehouse and set up a distribution agency in nearby Andover, although all of the spares are distributed from here at Flints Farm. The machines are a combination of road legal ATVs, a range of 50-250cc cruisers and small capacity fun bikes which are sold through our network of 150 dealers; by 2003 we were selling about 2000 units per year."

A good start, and in the last couple of years things have moved on at a pace. They now have their own company in China, making a bike using the best components from outside suppliers – enter the CR3. A sportingly styled, 125cc single cylinder 4-stroke featuring twin disc brakes, 5-spoke cast wheels – and, perhaps more importantly, the first road bike for over forty years to carry the name of AJS.

How things might develop is anyone's guess, and who knows what the future holds for the once famous name? But rest assured, given the Browns' enthusiasm AJS is far from dead and buried.

It was a great pleasure to spend the day charting the last fifty years with Fluff and Nick; many thanks to them for their time and hospitality.

With *World of Sport* trophy winner Arthur Browning in 1972. (Photo Morton's archive)

Bryan on his 500 Triumph at the Lanc's GN at Cuerdon Park in 1958.

CHAPTER 9

Wearing the distinctive number 70 on his factory-supported bikes, Bryan Sharp was at the pointy end of 1950s and '60s off-road riding, and along with brother Triss enjoyed a whole host of successes in scrambles and international six day trials.

BRYAN SHARP - THE STORY OF NUMBER 70

It was at Willoughby Hedge on a bitterly cold day in April 1951 that a young man from Poole, still several months short of his sixteenth birthday, made his scrambles debut – his name: Bryan Sharp. For Bryan it was an eventful and memorable occasion, and despite suffering a broken front brake cable he brought his BSA Bantam home a creditable third in the 125cc race: a crisp £1 note – enough for four gallons of petrol – as reward for his endeavours. It was a promising start, although little could he have imagined that ten years later he would be a works rider competing against the best in the world, or be racing in front of 90,000 people at the Czech motocross GP.

On his immaculately prepared Francis Barnett, Greeves and Triumph's Bryan was just one of a sextet of international quality riders comprising himself (70), brother Triss (71), Jerry Scott (72), Derek and Don Rickman (73 & 74) and Ivor England (75), known affectionately by '60s scrambles fans as the 'roaring seventies'. I first saw him in action at a Westbury-sub-Mendip event in 1961, his distinctively fast but silky smooth riding style one which, in over 15 seasons of competition, earned him a staggering 438 scrambles wins, 6 international six days gold medals, 4 three day golds, 7 victories in American desert races and 87 one day trials awards. Later there was also success on four wheels, and although he never won a major scrambles title there can be little doubt that B A Sharp was one of the most talented riders of his generation. To find out more I met him at his home overlooking Poole harbour, where we spent several hours reliving some of scrambling's halcyon days.

That both Bryan and Triss should race motorbikes was not surprising, as pre-war their father Triss Snr was a top leg–trailing rider – and later captain – of both the New Cross and Crystal Palace speedway teams: Pops, as he became known, also road-raced at Brooklands, so bikes were around the Sharp boys from an early age.

"Immediately post-war dad made a bike up for Triss and me to ride around the garden: this 'TS special' featured a 2-speed lawnmower engine and a pair of shortened girder forks in a tubular frame."

The TS obviously gave Bryan a zest for speed because twelve months later, aged eleven, his name first appeared in print – a press cutting which, thanks to his meticulous filing and archive system, he still has to this day.

"We lived in Croydon and dad was friendly with Joe Francis, who owned Brands Hatch. This was in the days before it became a road-race circuit. He [dad] had an ex-paratroopers Welbike, and I got my name in

On his 250cc works Francis Barnett, Bryan won the 350cc race at Matchems Park in the 1958 Hants GN.

"THERE CAN BE LITTLE DOUBT THAT B A SHARP WAS ONE OF THE MOST TALENTED RIDERS OF HIS GENERATION"

In action on the 500cc Triumph at Tweseldown in the southern Scott scramble, 1959.

Off-Road Giants!

the papers after they found out that I'd lapped the Brands grass circuit at 32mph on the little Corgi."

Big brother Triss had made his scrambles baptism at Matchems Park on a James in 1950 although by the time April 1951 came around both Sharps were mounted on BSA Bantams.

"Triss' Bantam was an ex-road-race bike, and compared to mine it fairly flew. The funny thing was that irrespective of how many times we rebuilt them, mine was always the slower of the two. When you consider it was probably only turning out about 4 or 5bhp in the first place a slight loss of power was a big disadvantage, especially at somewhere like Bulbarrow where I had to push it up the steepest hill."

The Sturminster Newton club's circuit at Bulbarrow was a demanding and often slippery one, and it was there in September 1951 that Bryan registered his first win. His mount was a newly acquired 197cc James, which he slithered to victory in the muddy 1000cc handicap race – his £4 in prize money bringing the season's total winnings to £17 15s 0d, and described by Bryan as "the highlight of the year."

1951 had been a good year for the young Sharp, and his promise had not gone unnoticed. At the season's end he was awarded 3rd best novice in the Pinhard trophy, a prestigious award presented annually to promising youngsters aged 21 or under.

The winter of '51/'52 saw Bryan in trials action, firstly on a 125cc James and then a Dot. As he told me, it heralded the start of three happy and successful years on the Manchester-made 2-strokes, so much so that by the age of 18 he was a fully fledged member of the works scrambles team.

"People like Bill Baraugh and Terry Cheshire were really flying on the works Dots, and our local man Dennis Kelly was also going well on one, so dad decided to buy a trials 200cc. Although it had a rigid rear end this was a bolt-on type, so we dispensed with that and had it converted to a Burns twin shock swinging arm. This was a sturdy jig built unit complete with a rear mudguard made by an engineer near the old Croydon airport, although at that time Bill's works scrambler still had a rigid rear end."

During 1952 and '53 Bryan put in some stirring rides on the little 2-stroke, including the 200cc Sunbeam point-to-point, where he finished second and in doing so split the works pairing of Baraugh and Vincent. That performance earned Bryan works sponsorship from Dot, although this amounted to help with parts and spares and no money. He continued to ride the works bike, and on one memorable occasion beat his mentor Baraugh by a wheel in the British Experts at Redditch, although often a toss of a coin decided who rode which bike. It was a win described by Bryan as "My best ever performance on the Dot."

Bryan was called up for national service in 1954, although his position with the Royal signals at Ripon was conveniently close to the Dot factory, and it did little to hinder his burgeoning scrambles career.

The Sharp brothers were attracting other factory interest, and in 1955 Ernie Smith lured them away to Francis Barnett. A standard Barnett would only turn out a fairly modest 8 or 9bhp and 2-stroke tuning was regarded very much as a 'dark art' but compared to the opposition the Sharp's bikes were 'flyers'. This was largely attributable to the skilled hands of their father, Pops, who was regarded as a bit of a guru in racing circles for his ability to extract an extra 25 per cent of power out of the little Franny B. In reality much of this was down to painstaking preparation, and the talk in the paddock was 'spin the wheel on a Sharp prepared bike and it will keep turning longer than the rest.'

There were numerous wins on the Barnett throughout '55 and '56, but Bryan was also getting adept at riding the bigger bangers and in 1957 got a works ride with Triumph. This in turn spawned his first trips to the lucrative continental meetings, although as he told me the 'gain' was sometimes at the expense of pain.

"Triss and I rode the Barnetts in the Swiss GP (where I got a puncture), in Belgium and then on at Imola. I can't remember much about the race but recall that Triss got food poisoning and I had to get him out of hospital so he could get his start money. I started going to the continental meetings with Arthur Harris and discovered that at some they paid you decent start money but little prize money, or sometimes it was the other way around. We were at a meeting in France and in the 2nd race I got my foot jammed under the footrest – I was in lots of pain but decided to go out in the third race to qualify for my pay packet. I couldn't brake properly but I managed to finish 2nd overall. Arthur had to drive all the way back home and when I went to hospital they discovered I'd broken my leg."

1958 saw the Francis Barnett team of Bryan, Triss and Ernie Smith in Garmisch Partenkirchen for their first ISDT, in which both Sharps would win gold, for Bryan the first of six in the event he describes as:

"The most enjoyable in all my motorcycling. I recall that the first day was very wet and we arrived at one particularly steep hill where there was huge logjam of riders trying to force their way up. I noticed another steep track to the side, so Triss and I zigzagged our way up and bypassed the queue which included Brian Stonebridge on his Greeves, who had started before us."

As recognition for winning their gold medals Francis Barnett awarded Bryan and Triss with sets of gold cufflinks, but by '59 the works scramblers had gone over to AMC's own engine, which prompted a change to Greeves.

"While Barnett was using the Villiers engine it was a good bike which both went and handled pretty well. For some reason it then decided to change to its own 250cc AMC unit, and although it turned out slightly more torque and power it was plagued with overheating problems. The final straw was when I was at the Glastonbury, Wick Farm circuit for the Somerset GN, and in practice the Barnett seized. Dad had become a Greeves agent, so as you can imagine Derry Preston-Cobb had been badgering us to ride for it, but up until then we'd turned him down. Dad had a Greeves in the back of the van so I asked the organisers if it was ok for me to race it, to which they agreed. I'd never sat on it, let alone raced it, but went out and won the lightweight race from Joe Johnson and Pat Lamper on his Dot. The following week I got a phone call from Preston-Cobb saying 'just got the paper, I see you won the race on a Greeves – is that right?' When I confirmed it was, 'Cobby' laughed down the phone for a minute or more and from that point on (1959) I rode for Greeves."

It was the start of six very successful – and mostly happy – years between Bryan and the Greeves factory, which not only saw him notch up numerous wins both at home and abroad, but also add further medals to his tally of international six day golds. He was also going well on the works Triumph, but unlike Triss' bike which sported a BSA frame, Ariel swinging arm, Norton forks and a Manx front brake, Bryan's was a very standard machine.

"The frame used to whip and the forks constantly flexed, but it

Dicing with Jeff Smith's BSA in the 250cc Hants GN, Matchems Park, Easter 1963.

"I MANAGED TO FINISH 2ND OVERALL. ARTHUR HAD TO DRIVE ALL THE WAY BACK HOME AND WHEN I WENT TO HOSPITAL THEY DISCOVERED I'D BROKEN MY LEG"

Off-Road Giants!

Negotiating a Welsh bog on the 250 Greeves in the 1964 two day trial, in which he won gold.

was something that you got used to. The Triumph factory never had any real interest in scrambling so we were left pretty much to our own devices, and we did all of our own mechanical work on the bikes. There was never any real money in it, but for attending a trade supported 'national' Triumph paid me about 4d a mile travelling expenses plus a small bonus for a result."

Bryan certainly had some stirring rides on the big twin, and was a firm favourite with the continental organisers and fans – fans that sometimes went to extraordinary lengths to help him overcome problems.

"Arthur and I were at a meeting down in the south of France near Bordeaux when my gearbox went. There was little or nothing I could do so they put a request out over the tannoy asking if there was anyone in the crowd with a Triumph road bike. This French chap came forward and between races we stripped the gears out of his bike, transferred them into my scrambler and at the end of the meeting changed them back again – just for good measure I won the race."

Sharp and Harris were also two of the first British riders to race in Finland, but in the autumn of 1960 a chance meeting with Tim Gibbes saw Bryan embark on a six-month adventure to America.

"I was on the Greeves stand at the motorcycle show when Aussie Tim Gibbes came along and asked me if I fancied going to California to race. I can't imagine why he asked me but I liked the sound of it, so 'Cobby' hastily organised Greeves' agent Nicholson Motors to send me an official invitation and I went off to the US embassy to get my visa. I went home and told my parents 'I'm off to America on Monday,' collected my riding gear, and the following week I was bound for California, although at that time I hardly knew where it was. Greeves had just brought out the square barrel, so air-freighted one to Nicholson's to fit on the bike it had organised for me. They met me on my arrival and told me that two days later I was due to take part in the 'Rams' hare and hounds desert race – something which, as I quickly found out, was very different to an English scramble. There were several hundred riders lined up across the desert and when I asked which way I had to go I was told to 'follow that smoke bomb' and then colour dye on the sand. Just before the start my 250cc Greeves seized so Nicholson forfeited his ride and gave me his 200. The start was mayhem and I went over the handlebars but kept going, and by the end of the race – won by Bud Ekins on his 650cc Triumph – I was tenth overall and first in the 250 class."

It was a great start for Bryan and he would notch up six more victories on the Greeves, although in the famous Big Bear he was thwarted when, with half an hour to go and in a strong twelfth place, his clutch packed up.

"The bikes used for the desert races were mostly big twins with very wide 19in front tyres and no mudguards – when I asked Bud why this was, he answered 'no mud'. Racing at that time in America was very much an amateur sort of thing with little or no money. Nicholson supplied the bikes and a car for me, but I financed my stay by doing some cash-in-hand repairs at bike shops, showing slide shows to local bike clubs, painting Bud Ekins' house and erecting the grandstand in Pasadena."

On returning to England, Bryan brought with him some special valve springs which gave his Triumph a bit of extra urge, but '61 saw him in search of 250cc European (world) championship points with team-mate Dave Bickers. They travelled thousands of miles together through some fairly inhospitable countries, although getting out from behind the Iron Curtain was, as he revealed, sometimes more of a problem than getting in.

"Poland was a particularly dour sort of place, and it was a nightmare trying to find fuel stations. After we'd finished the GP we arrived back at the Czech border but the guards wouldn't allow us out of the country. It seems that it was compulsory to have your passport signed at each place you stayed, and as ours wasn't stamped we had to drive all the way – several hundred miles – back to Katowic before they would let us leave the country."

Chasing both European championship points and ISDT medals, Bryan would have many more memorable escapades in Eastern Europe which could fill numerous pages. However we'll limit ourselves to the selector's controversial choice of Trophy team for the '64 ISDT in East Germany – one which didn't include the name B A Sharp or a 250 Greeves.

As had already been displayed by the all-conquering Czech and East Germans – plus the likes of Stonebridge and the Sharps – lightweight quarter-litre 2-strokes represented the ISDT future. However, despite his previous superlative performances on the Barnett and Greeves – ones which had netted five gold medals – there was

BRYAN SHARP – THE STORY OF NUMBER 70

a stubborn resistance by the British selectors to include 250s in the Trophy team, and after being snubbed yet again in '64 Bryan refused to ride in the Vase team. This had the knock-on effect of causing ructions at Thundersley, as he was also due to represent Greeves in the prestigious Valli Bergamo enduro: although sympathetic, Bert Greeves told him that if he didn't ride in the ISDT then he couldn't ride in Italy. Eventually a compromise was reached and he rode in both, but having a point to prove he won each motocross hill-climb, every special speed test, and emerged as best 250 – a performance which helped the Greeves team scoop the coveted Valli trophy. Just to rub salt into the selector's wounds, in the September ISDT both Sharp brothers came away from East Germany with gold medals, with Bryan fourth in the highly competitive 250cc class, his earlier decision fully vindicated.

For the 1965 ISDT in the Isle of Man both Bryan and Triss lined up in the Trophy team, although the event is now remembered for the atrocious weather, which saw only 82 of the original 299 starters finish, and the controversy surrounding the Sharps' decision to retire at the beginning of day five, despite the fact that other British team members had already pulled out.

"The weather was awful and a lot of the time we were manhandling our bikes out of bogs and over stone walls, a situation not helped by the ACU's decision to specify that we all use trials tyres. The back-up was a shambles, and while the likes of the East Germans had all their support team in contact with walkie-talkies and supplied all the riders with hot soup and dry gloves at each check point, for us there was often nothing. We arrived at the lunch stop at Douglas – absolutely soaking wet – to find the British management team sat down in a hotel eating lunch. In some parts of the course we spent more time carrying the bikes than we did riding them; the mudguards broke off and we were riding virtually blind. I remember crashing and got up unable to work out which way I was supposed to be going."

Enough was enough. Not only did Bryan and Triss retire at the start of day five, but they voiced the reason behind their decisions to the press – something which did not go down well within the halls of the ACU or at Thundersley. Despite the fact that many ordinary fans and also well respected journalists like American Lynn Wineland wrote letters in support of their actions, the controversy brought the curtain down on both the Sharps' ISDT career and the works contract with Greeves.

On a brace of Metisses – a Triumph and a 200cc Bultaco loaned by the Rickmans – Bryan continued racing up to the end of '66, when after a spill he decided to retire.

"It was a scramble near Plymouth, and following a crash on the little Bulto I ended up in Derriford hospital when the clutch lever went through my thigh. I'd raced for fifteen seasons with very little in the way of injuries, but by then my career was on the wane so I decided to call it a day."

It wasn't quite the end of the Bryan Sharp racing career, because he had five successful seasons racing formula Ford single seaters. This included pole position at Hockenheim in the European championship, and winning the south west formula Ford title – a championship which had eluded him for so many years on two wheels, eventually won on four.

In the brake test at the 1964 Welsh, Bryan is closely scrutinised by ACU official Vic Anstice.

The Kendall brothers pose for Gordon Francis' camera in 1962.

During the 1960s sidecar trials were immensely competitive, with several top pairings battling for honours. One of the most successful was the Kendall brothers.

CHAPTER 10
KEN KENDALL

Some trials riders were instantly recognisable by their stance, style or idiosyncrasies, but it was said of the Kendalls you usually heard them before you saw them. The noise, however, was not that emanating through the barking exhaust of their trusty HT 5 Ariel, but through the mouths of the pilot and his passenger, shouts which to the uninitiated could easily be mistaken for a full scale argument. Sometimes ones of anger, but usually cries of encouragement between Ken and his brother Des as they fought to keep the snorting Ariel moving upward and onward. For the Wessex centre 'Barrow boys' it was a strategy which worked wonders, and in a golden era for sidecar trials against some formidable opposition they won no fewer than twenty-nine nationals. In addition to their numerous Wessex wins, the brothers were twice runners-up in the British championships and finished ten marks clear of their nearest challengers in the 1963 British Experts, a victory cruelly snatched away by an overly zealous official who disqualified them for having a defective speedometer.

To find out more about his successful fifteen years of trialling and that controversial disqualification, I met Ken and his wife Doris at their West Country home where we talked about his career.

Ken's mother's family was well known in the Bristol area as a breeder of horses, but as he explained, his uncles swapped saddles for those of much more exciting steeds.

"My five uncles Reg, Ken, Bill, John and Leslie Lewis all rode motorbikes, so they were in my life from an early age. Reg had the contract to look after the Speedway bikes at Bristol, so after school I used to go down to the track at Knowle helping to clean them and fill the fuel tanks with methanol.

Both Reg and Ken became very accomplished sidecar grass-track racers, and I made my racing debut when I was only fourteen years old. We were at Farleigh, and for some reason Reg's regular passenger didn't turn up so he asked me if I'd like to act as ballast. It was great, and I didn't need a second bidding when he needed me again later that same season for a meeting near Ringwood. I absolutely loved it, so much so that I made the decision there and then that when I was old enough I would get a bike of my own."

Ken yearned for a motorcycle, but this was in the days before schoolboy sport, so he had to wait patiently for his sixteenth birthday. In the meantime his zest for speed was satisfied racing in cycle speedway; a sport in which the name of K R Kendall regularly featured in the

A tight manoeuvre for the Kendalls in the 1962 West of England trial.

Making a difficult climb look easy in 1964.

Off-Road Giants!

results. He entered the world of work as an apprentice engineer with Bristol Commercial vehicles and soon had his first motorcycle.

"I had an accident at work in which I almost lost a finger and with the compensation money I bought myself a Triumph Tiger 80. I really fancied a go at trials, so after about a month I sold the Triumph to my brother Jim and got myself a 350cc AJS which we rigged up with a home-made sidecar."

It looked good, but its inexperienced constructors had given little in the way of thought to weight saving, as he explained.

"We made the sidecar frame and chassis and filled in the bodywork with some oak panelling; not surprisingly, it weighed an absolute ton."

Heavy it might have been, but with brother Jim in the chair Ken gave good warning of his potential by chalking up an award in his very first trial, a Bristol league event at nearby Keynsham. Throughout the winter of 1953/54 the brothers rode in several other local events including the March Cotswold cups, which gave them a taster for the nationals, the first of which was the D K Mansell – although this time not with Jim in the chair.

"I borrowed Gordon Withers to passenger for me, and thanks to him we ended up winning the 350 class ahead of Bill Howard who was a BSA works man. Having ridden regularly with Reg Lewis, Gordon was extremely experienced and talked me through every section. As you can imagine I was dead chuffed."

Like most young men of his generation Ken served the obligatory two years' national service, which put his trials aspirations on hold until 1956. They were two barren years away from competition, but not, as he told me, from planning and constructing his new trials iron.

"I was stationed at St Mawgan in Cornwall, but on my leave weekends I would return home to work on the Ariel HT5 outfit I was building. I came out of the RAF and could hardly wait to get riding again, but by the time the John Douglas event came around there was still some work needed to finish the Ariel, so I borrowed an outfit from Reg Lewis."

After two years in the services money was a bit tight and it was very much trials on a shoestring, but his potential had not gone unrecognised.

"The John Douglas that year started from the Compass Inn at Tormarton, and as we lined up I was approached by the Shell rep Joe Gare. Joe could see that we were riding on a budget so offered to pay for six or seven gallons of petrol. This was our first form of sponsorship or support."

And as he explained, Shell wasn't the only one to recognise his talent.

"Bob Walsham and his sidekick from Avon tyres, Brian Heath, would be at most of the trade supported events, Brian took one look at my back tyre and said 'that's not going to last, I think we'd better do something for you.' Something they did until 1960, when Avon withdrew from competition support; certainly during those four years they were very good to us. We also had some support from both Reynolds and Girling, and shortly after Avons pulled out we were signed by Dickie Davis to ride on Dunlops."

There were few trials when the name of the Kendalls and the Ariel didn't figure in the results, although as I learnt the passenger duties had now been taken up by youngest brother Des.

"Jim had also been called up for national service where he managed to get into the Royal Corp display team, so at fifteen Des took over as my passenger. From the outset we shouted a lot and got some strange reactions from fellow competitors, observers and spectators as we rode the sections bellowing at each other!"

Along with Ken's then fiancée Doris, the brothers travelled the length and breadth of the country to compete in the British championship and trade supported nationals, in the process putting thousands of miles on their Morris Minor pick-up. Travel in pre-motorway days was, as Doris explained, often a long and cold experience.

"It was a bit of a squeeze with the three of us in the pick-up, which because the heater didn't work was usually freezing cold. In the depths of winter the windscreen would ice up, so we carried a wedge of wood which was jammed under the back of the bonnet to divert warm air from the engine onto the screen. Often Ken and Des would be riding on two consecutive days, so we would return from Saturday's event and they would be up until 2.00am cleaning and fettling the bike in preparation for the Sunday trial."

Throughout his career the hallmark of any Kendall machine was its immaculate preparation, although not all trials resulted in glory; Ken recalled an early Victory trial which ended with a mechanical disaster, but as it happened good fortune was smiling their way.

"We were going flat out up the third section when there was a horrible clattering noise and we'd dropped a valve. As luck would have it Ariel's competition manager Ernie Smith was standing on the section and asked me if I could get to the factory the next day. Due to work commitments I couldn't, but Doris drove up to Selly Oak on the Monday and it supplied us with a complete HT5 engine in bits for which it charged £10. Sammy Miller and Ron Langston were its two main factory riders, so although we were never officially works supported Ariel continued to supply us with spares and parts, albeit in a very quiet way."

Ken and Des also had a dabble at sidecar scrambling on a potent 600cc Velocette belonging to Reg Lewis, but after four or five events decided it wasn't for them and thereafter focused their energies on trials. With lessons learnt from the oak-bodied outfit, Ken constructed all of his own sidecars, including one for his brother Jim who also showed talent on three wheels. Sadly his blossoming career was put on hold while he recovered from two badly damaged arms, injuries sustained when his Barbour jacket got caught in a moving army lorry. It was a golden time for talented trials sidecarists, and every week Ken and Des were competing against the likes of Arthur Pullman, Roy Bradley and later on Ron Langston, a man who Ken describes as "a brilliant all-rounder and a gentleman."

Ken's talents as a constructor were also getting recognised, and during his illustrious career he made no fewer than forty replica sidecars; extra income which Doris recalled paid for the carpets in their first house. Doris was also very much part of the Kendall team, and in addition to the nine years she spent as treasurer to the Wessex BSSA, she was one of the legion of unsung heroes out in all winds and weathers observing. Perhaps, then, it is apt that Ken should pop the question at the end of a trial?

It was at Minety Vale and the popular Boxing Day trial in 1958 that they got engaged, the cup which Ken collected for his victory the previous year filled with punch to celebrate. Given this start, it's perhaps not surprising to learn that the day after their wedding was also spent at a trial. The venue is long since forgotten, but Doris remembers

Ken and Des in action in the 1965 Beggar's Roost trial on Exmoor.

Negotiating a stream on the Metisse in the 1964 Wye Valley trial.

Off-Road Giants!

it for observing in her new sheepskin coat which got plastered with flying mud and wishing she could go home and give it to her mum to clean!

Ken had become an accomplished engineer, honing talents which would lead to many tie-ups with the motorcycling world, including helping Don and Derek Rickman with the jigs on the first Metisse and the manufacturing of the cams for Phil Crumps speedway engines. In time he would found the engineering company which now employs 32 people. With the Rickman association in place, he pensioned the Ariel off in 1962 for a Metisse which he would ride for the next two productive seasons. He was setting the world of sidecar trials alight with his riding ability, but laughed as he recalled a stray dog-end which almost did the same to the outfit and pick-up.

"We were coming back from competing in the Victory trial and couldn't understand why traffic was coming the other way waving and flashing their lights. We pulled up for petrol and had barely stopped moving when the chap ran out shouting at us to 'get that off the forecourt'; I didn't know what he was on about until I turned around to see the tarpaulin covering the bike was ablaze. We'd flicked a cigarette end out of the cab which on landing had not only burnt through the cover but also the petrol pipe which had melted and sealed itself. We were extremely lucky that the bike and pick-up hadn't exploded in a ball of fire. I was particularly narked to lose that cover, as it was the groundsheet from a tent an American soldier had given; a reward for finding one of their guns discarded in a hedge during the Second World War."

There was plethora of sidecar talent in the early sixties with probably half a dozen riders capable of winning a national, but a measure of Ken's ability was that he managed to win the Bath club's Knutt trophy trial some four years on the trot. Although all of the charioteers were out to win there was a great sense of camaraderie, personified perhaps when Ken came across Arthur Pullman stranded at the side of the road. With the Matchless out of fuel he towed him ten miles to the finish, whereupon he discovered that Arthur had beaten him to take the premier.

"The sidecar crowd were the best imaginable, and we would all have done it for each other," said Ken.

After winning the southern Experts in Hampshire, it looked like he'd made it a double in '63 when he brought the Metisse home first in the British, an event now remembered more for its controversy than the winner's exceptional riding skills.

"I can honestly say it was one of our best ever rides, so as you can imagine we were absolutely devastated to be told we'd been disqualified because our speedo didn't work. We felt that we had no other option than to accept it, so it really rubbed salt into the wounds when a couple of weeks later we were at a trial and met ACU chairman Vic Anstice. Vic told us that had we lodged a protest within the 14 day cut off we would have been reinstated as winners as it was a road traffic offence, not one which should have warranted disqualification. I already had my chin on the ground with disappointment so these were not words that we wanted to hear."

Ken now regards this rather philosophically as water under the bridge, although all of his rivals magnanimously agree that Ken and Des were the true winners that day in '63.

In the early sixties the Bristol area was a hotbed of sidecar crews all anxious to dethrone the Kendall's from their position as Kings of Wessex, and with the opposition closing in it was time for Ken to plan another bike. Enter the Kenman, a machine of his own design and construction which he debuted in the winter of 1964.

Fabricated from Reynolds 531, the frame which featured a large top tube containing the oil was described by Ken as being a 'cross between an Ariel and a Metisse' while motive power was taken care of by the well tried and tested HT5.

This at first glance appeared to be fairly standard Ariel trials mill, but closer examination revealed a special head and barrel, both been made by Ken, while hidden away inside the engine lurked some very special cams.

It bristled with innovation, and later in its evolution sported a manually operated front disc brake; one of the first trials bikes to feature such a ground breaking and trend setting device. It was a seriously competitive machine, and as the sixties progressed one which would earn Ken and Des plenty of silverware.

Twice they finished runners-up in the British championship, both times pipped at the post by Ron Langston – undoubtedly motorcycling's greatest all-rounder and a man much admired by his rivals.

Doris has documented Ken's fifteen-year riding career into several bulging scrapbooks, and there is barely a national trial where either the name of Kendall or Langston doesn't figure as best sidecar.

After fifteen successful years Ken's enthusiasm was starting to wane, and following a winter of inactivity due to foot and mouth he called it a day in 1968, although this is not the end of the Kendall involvement with sidecars. Des swapped his role to that of pilot and had two or three more successful years on the Kenman, and later Ken and Doris' son Robert became an accomplished motocrosser on a big bore KX 500 Kawasaki outfit, built and fettled by his father.

Nowadays, Ken keeps in regular contact with his old rivals through gatherings like the Victory dinner, and he laughed when he recalled an incident where he was mistaken by an autograph hunter for ex-world motocross champion Jeff Smith. Much of his sport is now centred on perfecting his golf handicap, a game which he describes as "the hardest," although his love for sidecars has not died.

Before I left, Ken showed me the immaculate HT3 trials outfit he's just finished building and also a big bore, short stroke HT5 motor featuring his own head and barrel. It might not see action up too many muddy sections, but come summer you can bet that Ken and Des will be doffing around the north Somerset countryside – although whether they will still be bellowing at each other is anyone's guess.

More water at the Trader's trial in April 1966.

"A MEASURE OF KEN'S ABILITY WAS THAT HE MANAGED TO WIN THE BATH CLUB'S KNUTT TROPHY TRIAL SOME FOUR YEARS ON THE TROT"

John in full flight on his favourite 500 BSA in front of the TV cameras in 1963.

Though he never won a major championship, John 'Burly' Burton was always there or thereabouts, mainly riding booming BSA Gold Stars; big machines which suited this big man.

CHAPTER 11
JOHN 'BURLY' BURTON

It was at the Wymswold circuit near Loughborough in 1952 that the 17 year old John Burton made his scrambles debut. On his old Jap/Triumph it was a tough baptism, but in a few short years the raw lad from the Midlands would develop into a top class rider, earning the ride of a works BSA and representing his country in the Motocross Des Nations team, racing against some of the best scramblers in the world. During the late fifties and early sixties the big man on the booming Gold Star would become one of the most distinctive and popular riders of his generation although, as he told me, those early races left him extremely frustrated and disillusioned. That John chose to race motorbikes should perhaps not be totally surprising, as pre-war his father 'Squib' was a formidable speedway rider for both Rochdale and Leicester – although his son's early introductions to motorcycle sport didn't leave him very impressed.

"When he was a lad my dad was very small, so his friends gave him the nickname of 'Squib' and it stuck – this, despite the fact he grew up to be well over 6ft 1in. The first meeting I was taken to was a speedway event at Sheffield, but I was frightened by all of the noise – in fact, I couldn't watch and sat it out in the car park. A couple of years later dad organised a trip to the TT where we watched the senior race from a vantage point on Bray Hill: the speed of the first bike – one ridden by a marshal – was unbelievable, and out of surprise I jumped back into somebody's garden. When the race proper started I was absolutely petrified by the speed and the noise, and ended up listening to it on the radio in a nearby B&B."

However, it didn't take the young Burton long to discover that riding and sliding a bike – a Corgi Welbike – about on his uncle's farm was a lot of fun, and shortly afterwards he saw his first scramble which prompted him to have a go himself.

"Dad and I went to Mallory Park to watch a grass-track, and halfway through there was a break during which they held a demonstration scramble. It was great and I decided there and then to have a go myself. We bought a rather old JAP-engined Triumph and I raced it a couple of times, but it was continually breaking down which was very frustrating, and it also made mother extremely cross. In fact it made her so cross she contacted Comerfords at Thames Ditton and ordered me a new bike. The BSA Gold Star was then the machine to have, so when she discovered that they had a new 500 Goldie scrambler in stock she decided to buy it for me and it duly turned up on the train."

72

"THEY SUPPLIED ME WITH TWO WORKS SPECIFICATION GOLDIES ... I HAD TO DO NOTHING OTHER THAN RIDE"

British team man John on the Goldie, competing in the 1963 Motocross Des Nations.

Dicing with Chris Horsfield at a TV scramble in 1963.

Off-Road Giants!

Armed with a new bike and the skills he had learnt from sliding the Corgi around on the farm, John was soon making a name for himself, and began to challenge his friend and mentor Dave Bowerman.

"Dave had already started racing before me and had become quite a useful rider in the East Midlands centre, so I guess it was a gauge of how much I'd improved when I beat him in the support race at the Lanc's GN."

In fact such was their domination the rest of the field was over a lap adrift, and the red-faced organisers were left apologising to the pair for not including them in the main race. In later years John would register many more wins at Curedon Park, but by the mid-fifties he was starting to spread his wings to the lucrative continental meetings.

"Dave organised all of the entries and we started travelling to the meetings in northern France in his A40 pick-up. They paid some good start money and we had a great time and gained a lot of experience, although the logistics of getting from Leicestershire to Dover, ferry crossing to Calais, practice and race plus getting back to work for Monday morning was all a bit fraught.

On leaving school I'd landed a five year apprenticeship with Humber cars in Coventry, and taking time off and skiving was severely frowned upon by my bosses. If you kept your nose clean during your apprenticeship the young journeymen were granted the freedom of Coventry. In reality this counted for little, but it meant that due to some charter from the Middle Ages I'm allowed to graze a herd of cows anywhere within the city."

Slithering around alongside Ivor England at a snowy TV scramble in January 1963.

The big man on the big BSA was getting himself noticed, and within three years he'd landed a plumb works ride with BSA.

"I was getting some good results on the Goldie, but it was all a bit out of the blue when Bert Perigo phoned me and asked if I was interested in joining the works team of Jeff Smith, Arthur Lampkin and John Harris. They were looking for a replacement for David Tye who was retiring, so as you can probably guess it didn't take me very long to say yes. They supplied me with two works specification Goldies which went back to the factory after each weekend's race for fettling and tuning. I had to do nothing other than ride."

1954 had been a golden year for BSA, with John Draper scooping the European championship ahead of Bill Nillson and Sten Lundin, while at home Jeff Smith had comfortably won the domestic series. The name of John Burton was soon being added to the list of winners, although it looked like his works days were numbered when his national service call-up papers arrived.

"Due to my apprenticeship at Humber cars I'd managed to get my national service deferred, and when I eventually went along I failed the medical. I'd previously crashed and broken my left wrist resulting in some poor movement, so at the medical I made a bit of a song and dance out of it. The doc decided I was grade 3. As national service was being wound down they were only taking grade 1 and 2, so I ended up not going."

The 'dodgy' wrist certainly didn't impair John's ability to control 380lb of bucking Gold Star, a bike ideally suited to both his physique and all-action riding style, a style that persuaded the selectors to include him in the 1959 Motocross Des Nations team.

"I can't remember much about the race other than it was at Namur and the British team won. I'd only got married two days before so the honeymoon had to be put on hold until after the motocross."

The British had a huge pool of talented riders all capable of taking on and beating the best in the world, so it was not a surprise that the line up of Smith, Don and Derek Rickman, Les Archer, Dave Curtis and Burton won again the following year at a rain-soaked event at Cassel in northern France.

John revelled in tough demanding circuits like Hawkstone Park, Shrublands near Ipswich and the citadel at Namur in Belgium. It was at Namur that he won his one and only GP, although as he told me there was little or no time to celebrate his victory.

"The GP was on the Saturday and us works riders were expected to be back home for the Sunday race at Shrublands Park. This involved travelling back through Belgium and northern France to Boloungne, catching a ferry and driving through London to Ipswich in the early hours of Sunday morning for the race later in the day. After missing a night's sleep we were knackered by the time we arrived."

There was no doubt that on his day John had the ability to

74

One of John's early races on the Matchless Metisse at a Frome TV scramble in 1964.

Off-Road Giants!

mix it with and beat the best in the world, and although he pursued championship points for two seasons he lacked that all important consistency and luck to mount a serious bid, though at the height of the Cold War his travels took him to some fairly inhospitable places.

"I did the world championships for a couple of seasons, travelling initially with John Draper and later with Gordon Blakeway. In addition to the win in Belgium I finished second in Luxembourg and had a few other good rides in Eastern Europe. Motoring to Russia, Czechoslovakia and Poland certainly put a lot of miles on the van, but it was a great experience."

The hugely popular TV scrambles brought the names of Smith, Rickman, Bickers, Goss and Burton to thousands of armchair viewers, although as the country slithered to a halt in the harsh winter of '62/63, John was racing on the other side of the world.

"Pretty much out of the blue I had an offer to go and race in New Zealand, where they'd organised a Triumph Metisse for me. It was a great experience, and at the end of the series I managed to finish second just behind Keith Hickman on his Cheney."

For all their attributes the works Gold Stars had seen little in the way of development to their chassis and suspension, and although Eric Cheney showed it was possible to shed over 80lb with his bikes ridden by Hickman and Jerry Scott, BSA itself was experimenting with a lightweight based around the B40. Brian Martin had taken over from Bert Perigo as competitions manager in 1959, although the lightweight singles – stretched to 420cc by 1962 – found little favour with Burton.

"There's no disputing that Brian got the C15 and B40-engined bikes really flying, but I just couldn't get on with them. The fact was I'm a big bloke and they were just too small for me."

After a promising start when Smith won the Hants Grand National in Easter '62, much of the lightweight's progress that year was marred by gearbox problems, so for John it was another season on the well tried and tested Gold Star. The Hants – traditionally the opening round of the British championship – was an eagerly awaited affair, although in '63 John's choice of petrol tank didn't go down too well with the BSA management.

"Both Smithy and Arthur Lampkin were on lightweight 440s, but I was sporting a red tank and front mudguard on my Goldie – this was for no other reason than a friend was making some fibre glass tanks which I'd agreed to test for him, and after a crash in practice I'd broken my mudguard so Derek Rickman gave me a replacement. There was nothing in it other than that, but the press thought I was snubbing my nose at Brian Martin because I didn't like the new bike. Typically they (the press) made a bit of a meal out of it, but I apologised to Brian and it was quickly forgotten about. Matchems was a championship round so we had to race there, but it was one of my least favourite circuits, as the whole way round you got pelted with flying sand and stones.

I had some great days at BSA and it always looked after me extremely well, but when it decided to halt production of the Goldie in '63 I had no interest in the lightweights, so it was time to look around for another ride."

Although perhaps by then slightly past his prime, John was still a very capable and formidable racer so there was no shortage of offers, but it was on an unusual Velocette Metisse he lined up before the TV cameras at Leighton in 1964. I remember watching this race and that it was a bitterly cold day. In fact, it was so cold I didn't fill the results out in my programme, but John recalls that the Velo engine was not ideally suited to scrambling and it was soon changed for a Matchless.

"I only rode the Velo a few times before changing it for a Matchless Metisse and then later for one powered by a Triumph Tiger 100. I'd ridded singles throughout my career but absolutely loved the power delivery of that revvy Triumph twin which was like the one I'd raced in New Zealand. I was still doing the TV events and racing a bit on the continent, but by then I'd taken over the running of the family garage and was generally losing interest. I recall that my last ever event was in France in the late '60s on a 360cc CZ. Arthur Lampkin asked me if I fancied going so I did, but I just couldn't get on with the CZ – everything seemed to be on the 'wrong' side – and I finished last out of a field of about twenty. I decided there and then I'd had enough and packed it in."

It brought the curtain down on fifteen successful years of scrambling, and although he never scooped a major championship John Burton was undoubtedly one of the greats of his era. For scrambling they were golden days, epitomised by the big man at 'full chat' on the big BSA.

Typical scrambles action from Gilo on the factory Triumph twin in June 1965.

For fans in the golden era of off-road motorcycle sport the names Giles and Triumph went together like fish and chips, salt and pepper or Laurel and Hardy. In scrambles, trials and international six day events, he became one of the top names of his generation.

CHAPTER 12

JOHNNY GILES - MR ALL-ROUNDER

It's the summer of 1965, and at Meriden the comp shop is abuzz with excitement and speculation. At the previous weekend's British motocross GP Triumph factory rider John Giles had finished a fine fifth and in doing so beaten many of the world's best scramblers. However, the word is out that Gilo's bike was a 'hybrid' featuring a frame from Triumph's fierce rivals at BSA. So how did Triumph react to this news? With a slap on the back or a slap across the wrists? To find out I spoke to the man at the centre of the controversy, Johnny Giles.

"It was obvious from racing against the BSA boys that the Victor frame was vastly superior to those on the works Triumphs, so Brian Martin asked me if I would like to try one. Unbeknown to the Meriden comp shop I slotted my works engine in, and after practising decided to race it at Hawkstone Park. It didn't take very long before someone twigged it was a BSA frame, and when I went into Meriden on the Monday the 'balloon' had gone up. Ivor Davies wanted to know how I'd come by it, and when I told him insisted I returned the bike to Meriden. I was then without a bike for a week, and on the following Wednesday Ivor told me to report to Mr Turner who wanted to see me. It was a massive office and I felt a bit like a bad boy being hauled in front of the headmaster. He said 'Mr Giles, do you realise it's an honour to ride a Triumph?' I said that it was, but to be competitive it badly needed a decent frame. However, Turner wasn't open to discussion and went on to say 'we're not interested in scrambles, we make sports bikes, in future stick to Triumphs.'"

That the Victor frame made the bike handle much better seemed to count for little, as fraternising with the 'opposition' at Small Heath was looked upon very seriously. An interesting attitude, especially when one considers that Triumph was owned by BSA, and – as history would record – also rather ironic that the following year the same marriage of BSA frame and Triumph engine would bring the Lampkin brothers gold in the ISDT.

Suitably chastised, Johnny departed, but unperturbed he continued to both ride and modify his works bikes right up until the comp shop disbanded in 1968.

Johnny Giles and Triumph: it was a long association which started in 1951, when Meriden sought a talented 'all-rounder' replacement for Bert Gaymer, who was retiring. They were given the nod by the highly respected Ralph Venables that a young man called Giles would suit their needs, and as the records prove Venables was a good judge. Over the next two decades he (Gilo) became one of the most successful and

77

Off-Road Giants!

An early shot of John on the twin in the Welsh two day trial. (Photo John Giles archive)

popular riders of his generation, and there was barely an important trial, scramble or international six days when the name of Johnny Giles (Triumph) didn't figure in the results. To chart that career – one which still continues to this day – we return to where it all started in 1946. Johnny takes up the story.

"Pre-war my dad had a BSA Sloper and sidecar, so when I was sixteen I got myself a 350cc BSA Blue Star. Angus Herbert was our local BSA dealer, and through him I got interested in trials. Angus was top man in the Owls motorcycle club, so naturally it was the one I joined. The club had some sections near Sevenoaks where we all used to go practising at weekends, but I had to wait until 1947/48 before competition 'proper' started."

Post-war Britain was an austere place, and as he told me the advent of petrol rationing brought new challenges, which called for some improvisation and lateral thinking.

"Our monthly ration of fuel was rather meagre, so we would ride to Sevenoaks, drain our tanks, and compete in the trial using methanol which wasn't rationed. Riding over rough and muddy ground certainly taught me a lot about machine control, and I also got to meet lots of interesting people."

Even at this early age John was looking for ways of improving the Blue Star, and he told me how an advert in the *Green 'un* caught his eye.

"I saw an ad for someone in Birmingham selling BSA parts, engines, frames etc., so I wrote him a letter – remember, very few phones then – and he replied saying that he had what I wanted and I could pay him on delivery. He duly arrived on a BSA with a box sidecar filled with a brand-new B31 engine, frame and forks, plus other bits and pieces for which I paid him thirty-five quid. Whether it had come out of the 'backdoor' at Small Heath is anyone's guess, but I married the B31 frame to the rear end from the Blue Star and converted it to trials spec."

It was on the new 'special' that John entered his first speed event at nearby Brands Hatch, a grass-track.

"It was in the days prior to Brands becoming a road-race circuit, and it used to attract all the top names like Jock West, Wally Lock, Eric Oliver and Jack Colver. I vividly recall the Irish coming over, and on their McCandless spring-framed bikes they walked all over the English team mounted on rigids. The circuit went in an anti-clockwise direction, and during the latter part of the '48 season I did about 4 or 5 open to centre meetings but always finished a long way back."

It was the end of a very short grass-tracking career, but the trials world was starting to sit up and take notice of the talented young man from Kent. Not only was he starting to win a few cups, but 1948 would see the start of a friendship with Gordon Jackson, a man who would go on to become a legendary works rider with AMC. It's a friendship which has lasted the best part of sixty years, and John recalled how they first met.

"I've got a feeling it was a Three Musketeers trial at Horsham when I first came across Gordon. There was a lot of deep mud and I recall that he had a 500cc Matchless on its side trying to get the chain back on after it had jumped the sprockets, so naturally I stopped to give him a hand."

Gilo and Jackson had a lot in common, not least the desire to become works riders, so they soon started to spread their wings and began taking part in the nationals – events which involved a lot of travelling.

"I'd managed to win a few cups but needed a better bike, so I bought a new rigid trials B32 from the BSA dealers G Tambridge in Tunbridge Wells. It featured an alloy head and barrel, and on it I managed to win my first national, the Bemrose, which was held near Buxton in Derbyshire. Normally Gordon and I rode our bikes to and from the events, but on this occasion I'd managed to borrow my dad's car and trailer. The ground was hard and snowy, but I had an early number and managed to finish on a clean sheet. As a result I qualified for the British Experts, but by the time it came around I'd moved on to a 500T Norton. I had a fairly poor ride and finished about half way down the entry."

By John's standards the British Experts might have been disappointing, but by the season of 1951 things were starting to happen. There were some extremely good performances, including the Stretham trophy where on the Norton he finished runner-up to Geoff Duke, and also on the scrambles scene where he was putting in some stirring rides. His scrambles career had started at Brands Hatch aboard the B31 BSA, a bike which featured a McCandless rear end, the Beezer initially doubling up as both a scrambles and trials machine – although for mud plugging the dampers were replaced by adjustable, non-springing tubes for a rigid rear end. His precocious talent had come to the attention of Ralph Venables, who in turn recommended

John Giles, Mr ISDT, poses with the factory twin. (Photo John Giles archive)

"WE DIDN'T HAVE ANY PROPER LIGHTS ... SO WE WOULD TUCK IN BEHIND A CAR AND FOLLOW ITS TAIL LIGHTS UNTIL IT TURNED OFF AND THEN WAIT FOR ANOTHER TO COME ALONG"

John flat out on the cub scrambler at Higher Farm Wick, Glastonbury in June 1960.

Off-Road Giants!

him to Ivor Davies at Triumph, a man who John first met at the 1951 Motorcycle show.

"I had a letter from Triumph inviting me to meet them at the motorcycle show in London. We talked about the bikes and they asked if I would like to try one. Obviously I said yes, so they arranged for me to go down to the West Country and ride alongside factory star Jim Alves in the Taunton clubs OTC Edward's trophy trial."

In fact, the Giles-Triumph debut ride went rather well, and when the results were published he'd not only beaten the established centre stars like the Jarman brothers, but also his mentor to take the premiership award.

"The following week I received a phone call from Ivor Davies asking how I'd got on and what I thought of the bike. We later met and Davies agreed that I could also have a scrambler, although he added 'we're not that interested in scrambling.' We shook hands, and right up until the comp shop disbanded in '68 we were held by that gentleman's agreement."

Giles and Jackson might have been works riders, but in the early days there were no luxury pick-ups or cars and trailers to take them to events, and travelling to a national trial bordered on high adventure.

"For an event like the St David in south Wales I would go to Gordon's house around 7.00pm on the Friday evening, and after riding all night we would arrive at Port Talbot in the early hours of the morning. We didn't have any proper lights so we would fit 'bobby dodger' torches on the bikes. These might have been just about legal but gave no illumination, so we would tuck in behind a car and follow its tail lights until it turned off and then wait for another to come along. Most of the nationals in Wales started from a colliery, so on arrival we would go into the canteen – this was open all day and night – have a cup of tea, and then sleep in a corner until 8.00am when it was time for breakfast. We would leave our torches and kit in the canteen, ride in the trial, and after more food and a shower ride back to Mick Dismore's mum's house in Aldershot. We'd kip down in the hall and return home after breakfast on the Sunday morning. We must have done thousands of miles riding to and from trials, and the only time we failed to get to the start was when a wheel bearing seized on Gordon's AJS."

For followers of the international six days trial the combination of J R Giles and Triumph became synonymous with British endeavour, and between 1952 and 1970 he won no fewer than 11 golds and 2 silver medals in the 'Olympics' of motorcycling. On his debut in 1952 Gilo was very much the new boy when he joined fellow factory riders Jim Alves and Peter Hammond for the ISDT, based around Bad Ausee in Austria. It was his first trip abroad, and as he told me one he was ill-prepared for. The original plan was that Bert Gaymer would bow out after the six days in the September but his decision to retire in the spring threw a spanner into the works.

"It came as a bit of a shock when Ivor Davies told me I was to ride in the ISDT, because it left no time to practice in the Welsh three day event – all I knew about the six days is what I'd read in the *Blue 'un* and *Green 'un*. At least with Jim Alves and Peter Hammond – entered on experimental 650s housed in Trophy frames – I had some experienced team-mates to show me the ropes. Of course, I'd given little or no thought as to how I might actually get to Austria, so when Jim asked me I said 'that,' and pointed to my 1939 Vauxhall 10, a car which had the back cut off to accommodate the bike like a pick-up. Jim's 'race transport' was an ex-post office side valve Morris eight, so with Peter, two bikes and me in the Vauxhall we set off in convoy for Bad Ausee."

While the Triumph team riders were expected to 'rough it' the five officials from the ACU travelled in some style. On arrival in Bad Ausee, Vic Anstice is reported to have said rather haughtily "the Triumph team will never make it, they're travelling like gipsies." However, despite many difficulties – including an incident when Alves had to negotiate a particularly steep mountain pass in reverse – the trio did make it. Sadly, it would not be a memorable event for Triumph, as on the fourth day Hammond only got to the first check before his gearbox failed, and Alves nursed his Trophy to day five before also retiring with a seized box. On the 500 Giles was still on gold medal schedule, but was thwarted by a flaking rubber fuel pipe which blocked the main jet. Difficulty in removing the ¾in nut from the bottom of the float bowl cost him vital seconds. The net result was that his richly deserved gold was lost by an agonising minute, and the only finisher of the Triumph squad had to be content with silver.

He might have been a works rider, but Johnny still had to hold down a day job – but with more time needed for motorcycling a decision had to be made.

"I'd started work as an apprentice with a Rolls-Royce dealership in Tunbridge Wells, but they wouldn't allow me the time off to ride in the ISDT so I decided to quit. I then got a job as an agricultural engineer. This not only gave me time off for motorcycling, but it also deferred my national service!"

By 1953 Johnny was really getting on the pace with his 500cc scrambler, and he and Gordon Jackson were invited by Folkestone Triumph agent Jock Hitchcock to race at a meeting at Lille in northern France.

"Hitchcock organised for us and the bikes to be collected at Calais, but when we arrived at Lille we were surprised to find that that the scrambles course was smack in the middle of the town and they were still bulldozing the big jumps. The organisers were anxious to attract a big crowd, so they got all of the riders together and told us to ride around the town and 'make as much noise as you can.'"

This obviously had the desired effect, because on race day a crowd of 35,000 turned up. The main race was a 35 lapper which saw Giles on the Triumph twin first past the chequered flag, with Jackson on the 500cc Ajay a close second.

The first eighteen months on the factory machines had seen the young man from Kent shine in trials, scrambles and the international six days trials. But when his national service call-up papers arrived it appeared that motorcycling activities would be put on hold and Queen and country were to be served in the Middle East – although as Johnny quickly discovered, the Venables influence stretched way beyond the inner sanctums of the motorcycle industry.

"As an agricultural engineer they decided that my skills would be put to good use in the REME, so I was told to report to Blandford for my first six weeks training. Trouble was brewing in the Middle East, so before I was packed off to Egypt I had to serve another two weeks training at Arborfield near Reading. I'd already been selected to ride for the south eastern centre in the inter-centre team trial at Rodborough Common (Stroud), but it looked my chances of competing had been well and truly scuppered. Venables was our team manager, and told me not to worry as he knew the Colonel and would get something sorted out. Despite being a civvy he had lots of influence, and after telling

Another cub, this time the trials version at the Trader's trial in 1962.

Off-Road Giants!

John just keeping ahead of Don Rickman at the top of the Leighton course in June 1963.

the colonel that 'Giles has got to be released for the trial,' I was given a weekend pass. This started at 8.00am on the Saturday morning, and at the appointed time Ralph ushered me out of the camp into Gordon's van – waiting with my bike – and we were on our way to Stroud."

For the south eastern squad it proved to be a fortuitous intervention, and thanks largely to its two star riders it ran out comfortable team winner, Jackson taking the premier honours with Giles a close second. On the Sunday evening Johnny was dropped off back at the camp, and with only a week left for training it looked like the next stop was Egypt – however, thanks to further Venables intervention there was a last minute change of plan.

"Ralph used to organise Wednesday trials at Bordon and was friendly with the man in charge, Colonel Good. There was only a day to go before I was due to go to Portsmouth, when out of the blue I was told the plans had been changed. Instead of catching the boat to Egypt I was going to Bordon to work on motorbikes. I learnt later that Ralph had told Colonel Good 'John Giles is stuck at Arborfield; he ought to be sent to Bordon to work on the motorcycle section.' The colonel pulled a few strings and I duly arrived, only to be told by the Sergeant Major 'it's no good turning up now as we're just going on recess leave, see you in a fortnight.'"

John would stay at Bordon for his two years national service, happy ones for motorcycling, which amongst other achievements saw him become army trials champion, this after finishing runner-up to Brian Martin the previous year. In 1953 he was selected to compete for both the Vase B and Triumph teams in the international six days based at Gottwaldov, but an active serviceman behind the Iron Curtain was definitely a no-go, as he could have been considered a spy.

"It looked like I wasn't going to be allowed to compete, so both Triumph and Ralph wrote letters to the war office. I understand Venables said that I 'should be released to ride in the trial for the country.' In the end they agreed that I could be demobbed for two months although it would have to be made up at the end of my service – incidentally, this was later forgotten about. I had to hand my papers in to the War Office where I was debriefed, and then had to go to MI5. They also gave me a good going over, and told me what I should and shouldn't do and what to look out for in Czechoslovakia."

For the long trip to Gottwaldov, John and his 500cc Trophy travelled with Kent dealer Jock Hitchcock in his A70 pick-up. Sharing space with them in the Austin was Jock's factory development 150cc Terrier, and at Folkestone – and much to John's surprise – some unusual bartering material.

"Jock knew a lot of the local fishermen, and when we arrived at Folkestone he stopped and loaded up with ten boxes of kippers. I couldn't imagine what they were for but he told me that en route they would act as exchange for our night's bed and breakfast. True to his word, two boxes paid for bed, breakfast and evening meal in Germany, and on the second day we arrived at the Czech border. We halted in no man's land for Hitchcock to rearrange his cache of coffee and silk stockings – secreted in the door – before heading off to the Czech side. Here the guards examined the underside of the pick-up with mirrors on long sticks and scratched their heads about the kippers – eventually Jock presented them with a box and we waved our goodbyes. The rest of the fish went to CZ people that he knew and also to a school teacher and her husband. They invited us to their house for a meal, but fraternising with westerners was severely frowned upon so they were continually on the look-out for the leather-coated secret police, who were everywhere.

We were housed in a big 'accommodation block' and when we signed on at the Hotel Moskva HQ we were given a propaganda 'goody bag'. This contained a couple of bananas and an orange, so Jock collected them from the British riders and gave the fruit to the local kids, many of whom had never seen a banana before."

In his period report, Cyril Quantrill started by saying 'there has never been a better organised international six days trial than the 28th in the series' – a comment borne out by Gilo. It was also memorable for the victorious British Trophy team. For the Triumph squad, however, things didn't go quite as smoothly. Peter Hammond went out on day four with a holed piston, and on the same day Hitchcock was forced to retire after he ran out of time. Giles was going well and still on gold medal schedule until the afternoon of day five, when he also hit engine problems – another holed piston.

"I was well up on time when the piston blew, but I managed to limp to the finish just inside my three minutes without incurring any penalties. On the final morning I decided to give it a go and the bike started: on one and a bit cylinders it was very rough, but I managed to nurse it through the last 127 miles to the final speed test still on time. It was using a lot of oil, and I had to stop during the speed test to fill up. At the end it was all very much touch and go whether I'd managed to keep to the allocated speed schedule."

Gilo leads Jeff Smith and Dave Bickers at a Chard TV scramble in November 1964.

"1954 WAS AN EVENTFUL YEAR, ONE WHICH SAW HIM GET MARRIED, DEMOBBED FROM THE ARMY, PICK UP MORE ISDT GOLD AND BUY A JCB TO START HIS OWN BUSINESS"

Gilo back on his favourite 350 twin in the West of England trial in May 1963.

Off-Road Giants!

In fact, when the provisional results were announced Johnny had missed his deserved gold by a matter of seconds – remember, this was all timed with primitive stop watches – but after a protest from the British team manager his gold – the first of eleven – was reinstated, albeit after a wait of two months.

Back home in Blighty, John had to undergo a debriefing with MI5 before resuming his duties at Bordon, ones which as he recalled gave him plenty of time for competition.

"Once I got into army life I actually had a pretty good time. As an instructor I managed to get out of all the parades, rode in either a scramble or trial every weekend, and in one of Ralph's events on a Wednesday."

For Gilo, 1954 was an eventful year, one which saw him get married, demobbed from the army, pick up more ISDT gold and buy a JCB to start his own business. Along with his friend Gordon Jackson there were also numerous trips to the near continent to compete in scrambles, Giles and Jackson often featuring as first and second past the chequered flag. Occasionally they were accompanied by AMC competition chief Hugh Viney, a man who was very keen to sign John to the Plumstead ranks.

"Some people thought that Viney was a rather dour chap, but I got on well with him and he was certainly keen to see me mounted on an AMC bike. In fact he became rather pushy, and after a while told me he had built me one and it was ready for me to try out. Throughout my career Triumph always looked after me extremely well, but at that time I wasn't paid a retainer so I asked Jim Alves what I should do. 'I'll have a word with Ivor,' said Jim. This he did, and from then on Triumph paid me a decent retainer: unfortunately I never did get to sample the bike that Viney had built for me."

The sight of Johnny Giles aboard the Trophy twin, especially when on a full bore assault up a muddy section, was enough to stir the blood of any enthusiast. But trials were changing, and by 1956 – and much to his disappointment – Johnny handed back the 500cc twin for the bike he would ride for the next six or seven years, the Tiger cub. On a 175cc sleeved-down version Ken Heanes had won a gold in the 1956 international six days, but as John told me, its early days were dogged by unreliability.

"We had a lot of problems with big end failures and also with oil frothing and wet-sumping – this was after it had got very hot and the oil would be blown out all over the place. Often during a trial I would ride it through puddles in an effort to cool the crankcases. The funny thing was that you could stop the engine, and after it had cooled down it would start and run perfectly OK. Eventually the comp shop fitted a Perspex side in a crankcase and traced the frothing problem to a spigot on the side of the barrel. This was interrupting the flow of the oil, and was not cured until they fitted a bigger pump and altered the shape of the crankcase."

The engine reliability problems didn't initially enamour Gilo to the baby Triumph, although there was no disputing that with a skilled rider it could be a very competitive machine.

In '58 he won the Kickham and in the same year also finished a creditable fifth in the British Experts, although arguably his most emphatic win came in 1961 in the trade supported West of England trial. Having spent the summer scrambling the big twin – referred to by John as 'a right animal' – it was his first trial since the Scottish six days, and with a loss of seven marks he ran out comfortable winner

over runner-up Sammy Miller on 15. Other memorable performances included winning the Tatra trial in Poland, the premier award in the southern Experts and the 200 cup in the Scottish six days. During his long career Gilo competed in the highland classic sixteen times, and although he registered class wins in 200, 250 and 500cc capacities, it was not his favourite event, citing:

"Far too many rocks for my liking!"

The association with the little single lasted until March 1963, when he caused a stir by wheeling out another twin at the inter-centre team trial.

"I was losing my edge a bit on the cub, so Triumph let me have a 350 which I rode until the comp shop closed in 1968 and is a bike I've still got to this day."

John was much happier on the twin, and one of his best performances came in the '64 Scottish, where despite finishing 78 marks behind eventual winner Sammy Miller he won a well deserved special first class award. Incidentally Triumph team-mate Roy Peplow – who had previously won the event on a cub – also opted to ride a twin and with a loss of 75 finished just ahead of Gilo in the awards.

The bulging Giles trophy cabinet is also a reminder that he was a formidable scrambler, and one who – with a competitive machine – was more than capable of mixing it with the best. Sadly, as he explained, scrambling held little appeal for his bosses at Meriden, and he was denied the chance to race in the world championships.

"The comp shop was always run on a shoestring and there was simply no money or interest in developing a decent frame, improving the gearbox, or funding the cost of competing in the championship. The bikes were returned to the factory once or twice a year for engine refurbishment and for frame re-enamelling, but the rest of the time we were left pretty much to our own devices."

Much of the time small modifications were largely ignored, but the privateer's favourite – a marriage between the best of Small Heath and Meriden – was one which, as Gilo discovered, was severely frowned upon.

"Brian Martin had given me a Victor frame and on it I finished 5th behind Smith, Tiblin, Eastwood and Lampkin in the 1965 British GP at Hawkstone Park. When it got out that I'd used a non-Triumph frame – worse still, one from the 'opposition' – I was hauled before Edward Turner, who told me in no uncertain terms that they (Triumph) weren't interested in scrambling and that in future I was to stick to what I was given. The following week my factory bike – now with a standard Tiger SS frame – was returned to me, although what they didn't know was that I immediately cut it and put in an extra ¾in of tubing, which made it handle a treat."

A broken collar bone prevented Gilo from representing the British team in the very wet '65 ISDT, but the following year he was back in the Trophy team in Sweden, this time on a 350.

"I guess that in some ways I drew the short straws with the 350. It had to be worked very hard to keep on the pace, and I rode it virtually flat out for the whole week. That said, it was a lovely little bike and one which was impossible to blow up – it was still running as sweet at the finish as it was on the first day."

John came away from the 41st ISDT with more gold to add to his burgeoning collection, a performance which Triumph was quick to acknowledge in the following week's *Blue 'un*.

However, as he told me, the comp shop's preparations for the

John on his way to gold in the 1964 Welsh two day trial.

"WHEN IT GOT OUT THAT I'D USED A NON-TRIUMPH FRAME – WORSE STILL, ONE FROM THE 'OPPOSITION' – I WAS HAULED BEFORE EDWARD TURNER ..."

Off-Road Giants!

John shows off the factory TriBSA prior to the 1966 ISDT in Sweden.

ISDT owed much to 'make and mend,' and was all done on very much a shoestring budget.

"For much of my time at Triumph, Ivor Davies was the 'rider's manager' dealing with all of the money and expenses, and it was chaps like Henry Vale and Vic Fidler who prepared the bikes. Those machines selected for the ISDT would be just picked from the assembly line at random and taken to the comp shop where they would be stripped down, the QD stuff added, and then carefully rebuilt. We had new machines each year, but a lot of the registration numbers went back to bikes ridden in the late forties and early fifties by the likes of Bert Gaymer, Jimmy Alves and Allan Jefferies. Around midday the track would slow down for the lunch break, so Henry and Vic would walk around with their scrap box and select things which had been discarded. This was usually things like barrels with broken fins or frames with faulty brazing. It was a great outlet for these duff components, as back in the comp shop they would rectify the faults and then use them on the trials bikes – in effect, the competition department ran on virtually nothing."

Against the hoards of 2-strokes it was becoming increasingly difficult for the British to be competitive, and for the '67 event in Poland they (the manufacturers) withdrew their support. However, for John – privately entered on a Cheney Triumph – and fellow team members Roy Peplow, Gordon Farley and Jim Sandiford, the trip to Zakopane in the Tatra Mountains was not without incident. Their Ford Transit ran out of road and got straddled across some tram lines, and after extracting the van they were slowed by a defective fuel pump. In the best tradition of ISDT improvisation this was overcome by strapping a bike to the roof and relying on a gravity feed to fuel the vans carb. Once in Zakopane the quartet found themselves in more trouble when they disputed an extortionate bar bill, this settled only after they had been marched off to the local police station.

There was no doubt that the ability to think laterally and to improvise impromptu repairs were important assets for the budding ISDT rider, but what, I asked, him was the secret of his success in the six day marathon?

"It might seem like stating the obvious, but to win a gold you first needed to finish – it was no good treating it like a five-lap scramble, so both bike and mental preparation were very important. At around 1200 miles it was a long way, so it wasn't possible to practice; therefore you needed to ride with a sharp eye and with 100 per cent concentration. It was important to know your limit, but also to ride with a little bit in reserve; the history of the ISDT is littered with people who tried to ride at ten tenths and ended up crashing out."

In 1968 Triumph decided to close the competition shop, and although John retired from trials he continued to ride in both the ISDT and scrambles on the Cheney-framed machine that he'd first used in Poland. He eventually signed off from six days duties in 1970 in Spain with silver – the same way he'd started in 1952 – and he packed up scrambles the following year.

With his retirement in 1971, it appeared that the curtain had fallen on a long and highly successful career. However, as history records it was anything but the end. Old timers and past masters – the embryo which would grow into pre-'65 – scrambling had started, and four years later Gilo was back.

We now fast forward thirty years, and while the bones might be older, the poise and style of the man on the sweet sounding Triumph is unmistakable.

Johnny Giles – one of motorcycling's all time greats – is still racing, and judging by the smile on his face I think it's fair to say he's still enjoying himself.

Typical action from Ivor on the TriBSA at a Frome Valley scramble in September 1962.

CHAPTER 13
IVOR ENGLAND – SMOOTH OPERATOR

Though never a works rider Ivor England was a front-runner in late '50s and '60s scrambling, his smooth and unflustered style often seeing him first past the chequered flag. In a 14-year career, which saw him win eight southern centre stars, he was undoubtedly one of the best and most popular riders of his era.

The scene is Bulbarrow Hill in March 1963; the vibrant yellow of the gorse-covered Dorset countryside a welcome reminder that, after the dark months of winter, spring was on its way, and with it the start of yet another scrambles season. Despite the chilly north easterlies, the narrow lanes were choc-a-bloc with fans making their way to the Sturminster club's season opener; among them yours truly – an excited ten year old in his big brother's A40 van.

The knowledgeable crowd was eager to see if the Rickman brothers would wheel out the new MkIII of their all-conquering Metisse, and whether Ivor England could add to his tally of five southern centre championship wins. After a winter of trials riding to keep fit, Ivor was keen to renew his battles with the rest of the centre's top names, and he also debuted a new bike; a 500cc Triumph Metisse. Wearing his usual number 75, he soon gave signs that he was not about to relinquish his title lightly, and with his fans urging him on became embroiled in a titanic struggle for the lead with Triss Sharp and Don Rickman. With flying mud peppering the crowded hillside the trio frequently swapped places, but the younger Rickman was in scintillating form and eventually ran out a comfortable winner from Ivor, with Triss a close third.

In virtually any southern or Wessex event at that time it was a foregone conclusion that a rider wearing a number of 'seventy-something' would probably be first past the flag. Ivor was just one of a sextet of international class competitors known collectively by Len Scott as 'the roaring seventies,' also comprising Bryan and Triss Sharp (70 & 71), Jerry Scott (72), and the Rickman brothers Derek and Don (73 & 74).

On that spring day in '63 (and numerous times afterwards) I was lucky enough to witness at first hand Ivor's fast yet seemingly effortless riding style, although little did I know that, over forty years later, I would be reliving those days with one of my boyhood heroes. In a fourteen year career which saw him win eight southern centre stars, Ivor was undoubtedly one of the best and also one of the most popular riders of his era; although both then and now he is still extremely modest about his achievements.

To find out a little more I visited his home in the beautiful New Forest where he lives with Audrey, his wife of nearly fifty years, and I started by asking him about his early days. Although, as he revealed, motorcycling was not met with wholesale parental approval.

"My first road bike was a 2-stroke GTP Velocette which I bought at age sixteen and then hid in the shed, hoping that it would go

87

Off-Road Giants!

Ivor (centre) as a member of the winning southern team in the inter-centre event 1960 – Ron Baines receives the trophy.

'unnoticed'. Of course it was soon discovered, and there was a terrible uproar when my dad found out. What he didn't know was that prior to buying the Velo' I'd already had another bike which I kept and rode on the farm where I worked after school."

Uproar or not, Ivor kept the little GTP and it wasn't long before the machine control he'd learned sliding around the fields was put to good use in his first scramble, although as he told me he could have easily become a speedway rider.

"Speedway was my first love and every week I used to attend the meetings at nearby Poole. I really fancied a go, and thought my prayers were answered when I saw an advert announcing that trials for budding shingle stars were going to be held at Matchems Park. I turned up, but unfortunately so did scores of other hopefuls which made it impossible for everyone to get a ride. Therefore I turned my attentions to scrambling."

Speedway's loss turned out to be scrambling's gain, though as he lined up for his debut race at East Meon in 1955, little could he have imagined he would be southern centre champion three years later.

His first 'scrambler' was in fact a 350cc BSA trials bike that he bought from Percy Small motorcycles in Southampton. It had a rigid rear end, and the only concession to scrambling was a pair of knobbly tyres. He was raring to go, but unlike many of his contempories who had to ride their bikes to the events, race and ride home again, Ivor managed to travel in style.

Audrey had just started work as a mobile hairdresser – a common enough occupation now, but in the middle fifties something virtually unheard of, especially in rural Hampshire. Such was its novelty value, Ivor's then fiancée and her sporty little MG featured in a period magazine article on the new venture. Perhaps not the ideal car in which to change out of muddy riding gear after a days racing, but with the bike secured onto a home brewed trailer, one which solved Ivor's transport problem.

Incidentally, Audrey tells me that over fifty years on she still visits some of her original clients although sadly the car is now long gone!

As Ivor readily admits he didn't set the world on fire in that first season, but his smooth riding style was soon getting him noticed, and 18 months later he notched up his first win on a 500cc Gold Star. The Goldie also taught him a lot about the mechanical side of things, as he explained.

"The bike had previously been raced by Don Rickman, but for some reason the engine had been stripped and was in a box. Harold Wakefield told me that I could have it, but first I would need to rebuild the motor."

Wakefield was sponsor, mentor and friend to the Rickman family, and undoubtedly a man of considerable means, but he is remembered warmly by Ivor for his great enthusiasm and generosity, especially towards those riders representing the southern team at the hotly contested inter-centre events.

Throughout his career Ivor was usually racing one bike while either buying or building another, and with his reputation gathering force he was soon on a works specification Gold Star, which he told me about.

"At that time it was extremely difficult to just go out and buy a new Gold Star scrambler, so I saw Brian Martin at BSA who agreed to supply me with one through my local agent, Stocker and Shepherd. It featured alloy petrol and central oil tanks and was as near to works specification as you could get, but I still had to pay a whopping £303 for it; this was a lot of money in the late fifties."

It was on this Gold Star that he scooped the first of his eight southern centre championships, and although BSA might have lapped up the reflected glory there was never anything in the way of works support for the Hampshire rider. Despite his fourteen highly successful seasons the factory rides always just eluded him, and it wasn't just Small Heath who missed out on his talents, as he explained.

"BSA had its full quota of riders so I tried AJS, but had no joy, as it only seemed interested in riders who lived within a short travelling distance of the factory."

Disappointing to think that he was refused the chance of a works bike judged not on his riding abilities, but because he lived in the 'wilds' of Hampshire.

Like many of his contemporaries, Ivor soon joined those travelling to the lucrative meetings on the continent, although for a man used to hurtling around on a 350lb Goldie his debut on foreign soil was made on a very different sort of machine.

"If you got a top three position at a national meeting you automatically qualified for an international licence, and I got mine after I picked up a third at the Hants Grand National at Matchems

Ivor flying on the 500cc TriBSA at Bridport in 1960.

"I WENT TO OVERTAKE A BACKMARKER BUT HE DIDN'T SEE ME COMING, AND WE COLLIDED IN A TANGLE OF LEGS AND FOOTRESTS WHICH HAD ME OFF"

Ivor leads old rival Derek Rickman at his favourite Bulbarrow Hill in September 1962.

Off-Road Giants!

Park. Dennis Kelly used to race a lot on the continent and had an entry for a meeting in France, but as he was recovering from a broken arm he asked me if I would like to travel with him and take over the ride on his Tiger Cub. This was ideal, as it meant he could show me the ropes, introduce me to people, and I could get a feel for things. I can't remember much about the actual race other than I didn't get on very well with the little Triumph, but I do recall that we came home not only with the shared start money but also several rolls of carpet supplied by some local French firms who sponsored the event."

This started Ivor and Audrey on regular trips to mainland Europe, and during his career Ivor raced in France, Germany, Belgium, Switzerland and Spain, often in the company of fellow Brits Ken Heanes, John Clayton, Frank Underwood and the Rickman brothers.

For the Englands it was very much a team effort, and Ivor was quick to mention the huge support and encouragement he's received from Audrey.

"Throughout my career Audrey dealt with all of the entries, ferries and hotel bookings – all I had to do was ride the bike," he told me with a smile.

These continental meetings paid well, but invariably involved a lot of travelling, and for Ivor a long dash back home for Monday morning and work on the farm. Scrambling was hugely popular both at home and abroad, and on the back of the good start and prize money to be earned several of his fellow Brits turned professional; although for Ivor racing was first and foremost something he did because he enjoyed it. By the late fifties, the Spanish were getting into the burgeoning sport of motocross, and along with Don Rickman, Ivor was invited to the Ossa works in Barcelona.

"Through the ACU, Ossa had asked for a couple of riders to go out to Spain and help develop its bike ahead of the Spanish GP. Harold Taylor had organised Don and Derek Rickman to go, but Derek was nursing an injury so he invited me to take his place. Harold, Don and I were flown from Gatwick to Barcelona where we were treated extremely hospitably by the Ossa people. We tested the bikes on their track and gave them feedback on any alterations and modifications that were required, especially regarding things like the position of the footrests and handlebars. At the end of the week we raced them in the GP, which was held at an old golf course and lined by thousands of cheering enthusiastic Spaniards."

Ivor's name and success became synonymous with booming 500cc 4-strokes, Gold Stars, TriBSAs and, later on, Triumph powered Metisses, but the Ossa was not his only association with ring-dinging 2-strokes.

"I raced a Dot for a while without any great success, and then I was asked to ride a Greeves for Sid Lawton in the Moto-Rodeo. Speedway had gone a bit flat, so the promoter Charlie Knott came up with the idea of a series of arena races in Southampton. He attracted some good riders who were nearly all on lightweight machines, many of which were supplied through dealers who fettled and tuned them between meetings. It paid well, and I was getting paid as much racing there once a week as I did for three weeks' work on the farm."

Knott's events were a lot of fun for the riders but only of novelty value to the spectators, and they fizzled out after a season or so although, on reflection, they were probably too far ahead of their time.

Held at the popular Leighton circuit, the Frome club's August bank holiday Rob Walker trophy meeting was always a keenly contested affair, and for Ivor a happy hunting ground. The undulating course at Heal's ladder was undoubtedly one of his favourites, and following his third successive win over John Clayton in 1960 he retained the much prized silverware. This, along with an extra £20, was presented by its donor, the former Formula One race team owner Rob Walker, and now takes pride of place in Ivor's impressive trophy cabinet.

While many of his rivals displayed an 'on the edge' riding style of leaps and wheelies which resulted in the almost predictable crash, number seventy five was definitely 'Mr Smooth' and an England tumble was a rare sight. Fourteen years of racing brought the inevitable cuts and bruises, but an incident sustained while leading the Pirbright 100 miler was perhaps his worst injury and it also left a 'nasty taste in his mouth,' as he told me.

"As you can imagine, racing for that length of time was incredibly tiring and called for good back-up for refreshments, refuelling and the like. I pulled up to take on petrol and have a drink, but ended up with a mouthful of undiluted orange as someone had forgotten to mix it with water – it tasted ghastly. I was going really well and in the lead, but in the muddy conditions racing (and lap scoring) soon became chaotic and picking your way past riders flagging with fatigue was extremely difficult. I went to overtake a backmarker but he didn't see me coming, and we collided in a tangle of legs and footrests which had me off; my race ended with a visit to the medic's tent with a badly mangled leg."

Other incidents, however, had a happier conclusion, and Audrey recalled one from the quaintly named Grandfather's bottom, involving the late Phil Nex.

"The track at Grandfather's bottom featured some deep hollows followed by an amazingly steep hill which led onto the start and finish straight. It was a very foggy day and I was waiting at the pit fence when a very concerned Phil rode out of the race to tell me that he thought he'd ridden over Ivor in one of the hollows. In fact we soon discovered that Ivor had broken down, and when the race ended both him and the dead Gold Star eventually appeared at the end of a long tow rope hauled by a gang of about a dozen willing helpers. I think Phil was in the lead at the time, but it was a typical gesture of the man; a true sportsman."

From the late fifties onward Ivor competed in virtually all of the British national events, regularly picking up championship points for his efforts and usually mounted on machines he'd constructed himself. The Goldie had been pensioned off and replaced by a variety of TriBSAs and later on a Metisse which, befitting a championship contender, was towed to meetings the length and breadth of the country behind a 3.8-litre Jaguar. The TriBSAs went through a steady series of improvements before eventually evolving into the seriously competitive machine he campaigned in the early sixties, which he told me about.

"I loved the power delivery of the pre-unit Triumph twin engine but the standard Meriden frame was pretty awful, so the trick was to use one from a BSA. I also used a BSA gearbox fitted with a longer main shaft to marry up with a Norton clutch, which didn't slip like those on the BSA. The forks were Norton roadholders, but during the course of a race they would lose their damping so in the days before specialist products we filled them with oil, which was so thick it was more like treacle. The engine oil also used to get extremely hot, making the pump stick with catastrophic results, so I started to experiment with an oil carrying frame. I took the Beezer frame to a company in Bournemouth that blew it through with a high pressure jet, which removed all of the leftover swarf and muck. The end result was that the motor ran much

Typical smooth action from Ivor at an XHG Tigers meeting at Giant's Head in July 1962.

"HIS NAME AND SUCCESS BECAME SYNONYMOUS WITH BOOMING 500CC 4-STROKES, GOLD STARS, TRIBSAS AND, LATER ON, TRIUMPH-POWERED METISSES"

Off-Road Giants!

On his Triumph Metisse, Ivor leads Terry Cox at the national Wessex scramble at Glastonbury in April 1964.

cooler and I had a lot less in the way of engine rebuilds to contend with. The Rickmans used a similar idea in the Metisse, but this had an added advantage in that it was made of bigger gauge tubing which was less prone to cracking and breakages."

On his home-brewed machine Ivor was a member of the team comprising Don and Derek Rickman, Triss Sharp and Ken Heanes that scooped the inter-centre team championship in 1962. He was often at the end of micky taking and banter regarding his good looks, and as they lined up for the winning team photograph a fellow member was heard to quip "Ivor should keep his helmet on, 'cos he's too handsome when he takes it off."

With little doubt, the Rickman Metisse was the best 'over the counter' scrambles bike of its day, and the machine which Ivor would race from '63 until his retirement five years later. By then, courtesy of the hugely popular TV scrambles, his name had spread to a wider audience and there were few events where the name of England didn't figure in the results. These have been carefully documented in a series of bulging scrapbooks which could have kept me absorbed for hours. They frequently show reports of Ivor England, three starts, three wins; reports modestly referred to by Ivor as "not a bad day."

Undeniably, this modesty – added to his friendly, approachable nature and 'never say die' riding style – made him one of the southern crowd's favourites. Lifelong friendships were made from people who came along to say hello in the pits, including Jill and Cyril Harris who the England's met at Beenham Park in the early sixties. They were later godparents to son Nick, who would be the next motorcycle star in the England household. After learning the ropes around the family's garden on a mini 50cc Suzuki Metisse, Nick went on to become one of the southern centre's best trials riders. During the 1980s he rode both works Fantic's and Shirt Yamaha's to great aplomb, and the name of England once more appeared as southern centre champion.

I had a great afternoon reliving those days with Ivor and Audrey, but it's not just the fans and the '60s aces who remember him. One Sunday three or four years ago a stranger knocked at their door.

"You don't know me," he said "but about forty years ago I was a junior rider having problems with my BSA gearbox at a meeting at Glastonbury. You showed me what was wrong and gave me a new selector fork which fixed the trouble; I just stopped by to say thanks."

Ivor England – a true champion!

Ken on the factory TriBSA in the 1966 ISDT in Sweden.
(Photo Heanes archive)

Ken Heanes was arguably the greatest six days trial rider ever to grace the sport of long-distance trialling, scooping numerous awards over three decades. He was also a handy scrambler and trials rider, too.

CHAPTER 14
KEN HEANES – MR ISDT

The international six days trial was arguably one of the toughest tests for both rider and machine in the world, and not without good reason was it labelled the Olympics of motorcycling. The marathon that pitted the riders and their machines in a six day race against the clock, across mountains, through bogs, streams and forests, was perhaps the ultimate challenge of skill, endurance and mechanical durability. For the winning riders there was the prize of a gold medal along with the national pride and accolades that came from representing their country, while for the successful manufacturers victory brought a huge amount of publicity, prestige and commercial spin offs.

Both the *Blue 'un* and *Green 'un* devoted many pre and post-trial pages to this prestigious annual event, and as a result those who proudly wore the union flag became household names. In an ISDT riding career which covered three decades, Ken Heanes not only became synonymous with British success, his meticulous preparation and indomitable attitude also embodied the whole spirit of the event. To learn more about this long and successful career I visited him at his Hampshire home, where we were later joined by Alan Davey, who owns the Cheney Triumph WCG 101H which Ken rode to gold in Spain in 1970 and the Isle of Man in '71.

Much of Ken's career was spent riding Triumphs, but both his riding and competition debuts were made on vastly different machines, as he explained.

"My father Jim rode with some degree of success on Ariels in the 1930s, so as there were always bikes around I got interested at an early age. I was eleven when the war ended, and I would come home from school and secretly remove from the shed the 1914 flat tank Royal Enfield which dad was trying to sell – I think he was asking £4 17s 6d for it! At least I thought it was a secret, but he noticed that the milometer kept moving by the odd tenth of a mile or so and guessed that I was up to something. I would get a friend to push me up and down the track in the woods that adjoined our house and it wasn't long before I felt confident enough to try to start it. It fired up and quickly dispatched me headfirst into a tree, fortunately without serious injury.

Jim found this very amusing and decided that it was time that I had my own machine, so made me up a field bike which he pieced together around a WD type 250 Matchless. Throughout my career he was hugely supportive and gave me lots of advice, assistance and encouragement, but without any pressure. Certainly in the early days I

93

Off-Road Giants!

learned a great deal from him, especially when it came to hacksawing lugs off old frames and making up brackets."

These skills would be put into practice by Ken many times over the years, but after a couple of years on the Matchless he was developing a zest for speed and his first event beckoned.

"I loved dashing through the woods on the Matchless, so in 1947 aged 13 I entered my first event, a speed hill climb held at Buster Hill, Petersfield. I was ready for action but was bitterly disappointed on the day when the organisers decided that I was too young to compete (there was no schoolboy stuff in those days). At the end of the event – by way of compensation – they allowed me a 'demonstration ride' and to the amazement of all concerned I set the fastest time of the day. Some time later the club sent me a framed photograph and letter recording this feat, which I still have to this day."

Continued practice on the Matchless saw Ken notch up his first win in an evening trial, and shortly after at 15 he entered the world of work with an apprenticeship at Archers motorcycles, for which he was paid the princely sum of £1 a week! With an eye on bigger and better things he enrolled on a one day a week motor vehicle technician's course at Guildford College, and soon after his 16th birthday made his ISDT debut – although by his own admission he was "a bit green."

Typical Heanes poise at the Berks Grand National in August 1959.

"I was riding regularly in trials and scrambles on a BSA Bantam, 125 Royal Enfield Flying Flea and the old faithful Matchless when Jim's great mate and my godfather Jack Stocker told me we were going to Wales for the week and he'd arranged for me to have a semi-works Royal Enfield 350 Bullet to ride. Jack told me to 'just keep going' and by the end of the third day I was still clean, but shortly before the final check picked up a puncture in the rear tyre. It meant that I had just ten minutes the next morning to take out the non QD wheel and replace the tube before setting off again. After our evening meal Dickie Davies and his friend Tom (who incidentally were both quite drunk) from Dunlop's competition department volunteered to show me how to execute a speedy tyre change, and they took me off to the Automobile Palace in Llandrindod Wales where I practiced until my hands were red raw. The following morning I managed to replace the tube and went flying away at speed, but trying to get back on time I overcooked it and crashed headlong into a wall. The front end of the bike was much mangled, but thankfully I was uninjured and I remember that my first consideration was where's my cap? It was in the days prior to compulsory helmets and I was wearing a cheesecutter-style cloth cap which I later retrieved from a hedge. Obviously I was forced to retire, but it had whetted my appetite and I vowed that I would return and win a gold medal. My father rode in two events (1949/1950) and won silvers in both, although each time lost his chance of gold through talking and failing to start on time."

Ken had to wait for another six years before his next ISDT ride, but his dashing riding style was starting to get him noticed and by 1954 he was on a works Triumph twin, something which had a lot to do with lady luck, as he explained.

"I was at a scramble at Pirbright, and towards the end of the meeting Eric Cheney asked me if I fancied a ride on his Ariel. The race was the all-comers, non-winners race which I duly won, a victory witnessed by Ralph Venables. Ralph had numerous influential connections and recommended me to Ivor Davies at Triumph, who signed me up for my first works ride."

On the rasping twins Ken logged up many scrambles wins both at home and at meetings in France and Belgium, where he often travelled in the company of Gordon Jackson, Jim Sheehan and Ivor England in an Austin A40 pick-up.

By 1956 his ambitions to return to the ISDT and win gold were realised on a most unlikely machine, a sleeved-down 175cc Triumph Tiger Cub. The event which was based around the West German town of Garmisch Partenkirchen was particularly tough, and out of 313 starters only 111 made it to the finish, among them Ken on the baby Triumph. Not only did six days success call for meticulous machine preparation and a high level of rider stamina, it also relied on improvisation and lateral thinking.

"Triumph had just released the Cub and was keen to exploit its off-road potential, so it sleeved-down UAC 377 for me to ride as a member of the Vase B team. From the start I had to ride with its throttle flat against the stop, but the cub didn't take favourably to this abuse and by the first check it had partially seized. Jack Stocker was on hand with a tin of Molyslip in his pocket, and told me to stick it into the oil tank, which fortunately worked wonders. Some of the climbs were more like those found on a one day trials section, and the steep slots became jammed with bikes and riders and the only way to maintain progress was to wind the throttle open and slip the clutch. This harsh treatment

Spirited brake test from Ken in the Welsh two day trial in May 1964 – next stop, East Germany.

A member of the winning southern centre team with the Rickman brothers, Triss Sharp and Ivor England in August 1964.

Off-Road Giants!

eventually fried the clutch plates, and at the top of a particularly difficult ascent it cried enough. I wasn't about to give up, so I took a ball headed hammer which I had taped to the frame and knocked a hole in the primary chaincase and filled it up with mud. This miraculously gave the clutch enough bite until I could clear the hill and effect a more permanent repair. Replacement of the clutch was out of the question, so I made another hole in the chaincase until I could tighten up all the clutch springs solid, and rode the rest of the week with no clutch."

You might not think things could get any worse, but on day three the frame broke; although not deterred, the ever-resourceful Ken wrapped the spare chain under the frame tube and over the top of the tank to hold it all together. Day five saw the battery explode, but amazingly the little Triumph kept running and on the last day he was still on schedule for gold.

"Despite being ridden flat out from the first morning I'd kept it going, and all that was between me and my first gold was the last day speed test. I think the 175s had to average something like 56mph and by this stage the Tiger Cub was both looking and sounding decidedly second-hand. Triumph's competition manager, Henry Vale, was standing on the last corner, and as I approached him flat on the tank, the engine expired in a big way. I had to coast the bike across the line but I'd managed to win my gold medal."

This was the start of Ken's successful six days career which would see him represent his country as both rider and manager for the next nineteen years, and in the process net a grand total of 10 gold and 2 silver medals.

The Welsh three day was traditionally used by the ACU as a selection event for our teams, and it was in these that he learned much about machine preparation, as he told me.

"Bob Manns was undoubtedly one of the best 'spanner men' I ever saw, and someone who I learned a lot from when it came to machine preparation and improvisation. During the selection tests we would be stopped and instructed by ACU officials to carry out various tasks, like changing a tyre or throttle cable. Some would take ages to just get their tool kit out, but a totally unflustered Bob would carry out a tube change in a matter of minutes. The rear wheel would seemingly fall out, and where others were left struggling with security bolts Bob's tube would be changed and he would be on his way again. His secret was that prior to the event he would remove the pad of the security bolt and chisel mark grooves in an anti-clockwise direction into the rim, which would prevent any tyre creep but make for an easy removal. A similar ploy was used by the East Germans on their MZs, which featured angled grips welded onto the inside of the rim.

Not only was Bob Manns a very good rider, he was also adept at a bit of improvisation – like the time he had a pushrod break in the Welsh. This would have been enough to stop most people, but Bob extracted the broken rod from its tube and took his tyre pressure gauge apart. Fortunately the inside diameter matched that of the pushrod, and the splinted repair not only got him mobile again, it survived the rest of the trial.

When I got my engines from Triumph I would rebuild them so I knew them inside out, and then lock wire up everything that didn't need to be removed. I learned very quickly to standardise on bolt sizes and got it down to such a fine art the whole Triumph tool kit consisted of about three spanners. 80 per cent of success in the ISDT was down to machine preparation and the other 20 per cent down to mind over matter."

The 1960s were undoubtedly Kens glory years, and not only was he successful in both his ISDT and scrambles exploits, but also with his burgeoning motorcycle businesses, which by now totalled four shops. After finishing his apprenticeship with Les Archer he had left college with a plethora of City and Guilds certificates, and decided at 21 to start his own business, naturally becoming an agent for Triumph. He was soon supplying police specification bikes to seven forces, and prior to delivery would road test them himself – which led to the odd 'transgression' of the law, as he explained.

"The Hampshire police were having a purge on speeding and I got three tickets in a month, two of which were for riding police bikes at 34 mph in a 30 limit. I faced a ban so appeared in court, but after it was pointed out to the judge that 'Mr Heanes supplies motorcycles to the police and was testing them prior to delivery' was only fined £10. This was much to the chagrin of my solicitor, who had lost his licence for a similar offence."

When competing in one Welsh three day Ken had another brush with the law, which he recalled with much amusement.

"One stage was particularly tight on time, and I suddenly came upon an ACU official who stopped me with a 'puncture rear wheel' sign. While I was changing the tube I was overtaken by one of the Metropolitan Police riders who had started four minutes behind me. I set off again at a considerable lick and caught and passed the police rider in a stream which led directly into a 30mph limit, which I flew through at 80-90mph with the policeman in hot pursuit. I arrived at the control with literally seconds to spare, and when the copper drew up alongside I expected to have the book thrown at me, but he grinned and said 'I've always wanted to have a burn up in a 30 mph limit.'"

The Welsh terrain proved to be ideal practice for the ISDT, and prior to the East German event in 1964 Ken was approached and asked to pass on his knowledge to the American team, which included Steve McQueen and Bud Ekins.

"The Americans had some very good riders but they had little or no experience of dealing with mud, so we all went off to Wales together to find some. It was glutinous green slime that you needed to hit at speed with plenty of weight over the rear wheel, and after I demonstrated it once or twice I beckoned Steve to have a go. He hit at a great rate of knots, but the bike stopped dead and he disappeared headfirst over the handlebars. He got up plastered from head to foot in mud and with a big cheesy grin said, 'Gee, do you think you could show me that again Ken?'"

Throughout the sixties Ken continued to campaign a 650 Triumph in the ISDT and its smaller sibling in scrambles, which he admitted felt like toys in comparison to the big bangers. Triumph, along with the other British factories, withdrew its support after the 1966 trial, so the 1967 event in Poland and the following year in Italy saw Ken mounted on a Triumph Metisse as a privateer; sadly, both ended in retirements. Some pretty poor quality petrol was responsible for piston meltdown in '67, and in Italy he went out on the second day when the gearbox failed. This bike was later bought by Ivor Thick, and is presently undergoing restoration in Somerset by its present owner Roy Emery.

At the end of 1966 Ken had bought his works Triumph and mounted it in a glass case in the study of his home, but with no other bike on offer it was brought out of mothballs for the 1969 event in West Germany. Although hopelessly outclassed by the winning East German and Czech 2-strokes, Ken and his Home Counties team-mates of Peter

96

Splashing through a Welsh bog on his way to two day gold in May 1964.

"THE AMERICANS HAD SOME VERY GOOD RIDERS BUT THEY HAD LITTLE OR NO EXPERIENCE OF DEALING WITH MUD, SO WE ALL WENT OFF TO WALES TOGETHER TO FIND SOME"

Off-Road Giants!

On his Triumph Metisse, Ken holds off Dave Nicoll's works Matchless at Tweseldown in 1964.

Stirland and Jock Wilson kept going to the end and secured the much deserved team prize.

Over the years a considerable amount of rule bending and cheating crept into the ISDT, especially amongst teams from the former Eastern bloc, and during the course of our talk Ken told me many amusing stories, including an incident from Italy in 1968. While their MZs were being checked an East German official was spotted and reported for slipping a tin of marking paint into his pocket. The international jury took no action as the next day all of the scrutineering paint had disappeared necessitating the authorities to change the paint colour and remark all of the entries. In the haste to get everything repainted things inevitably got missed and didn't come to light until later, like the unmarked MZ cylinder head belonging to the East German Rolf Uhlig. Despite the feeling that fiddling had been involved, Uhlig was given the benefit of the doubt by the international jury, and following a vote was allowed to continue.

From the event's conception, the prestigious Trophy prize had been awarded to a national team riding machines manufactured within its own borders, but as the new decade dawned the rules were changed. The FIM decided to open the Trophy competition to all its members, thus enabling them to enter a team mounted on foreign machinery.

The days, however, when a thinly disguised road bike could be shorn with knobblies and called an ISDT machine were long past, and something specialised was needed to match the Eastern bloc 2-strokes. The ACU was keen to keep our Trophy team mounted on home machinery, but what remained of the British industry showed little interest, so the honour of flying the flag came down to Eric Cheney. Ken takes up the story again.

"With little or no interest from the industry, I managed to persuade five other large dealerships in the form of Elite Motors, Comerfords, Bill Slocombe, Jack Williams and Alan Jefferies (plus myself) to fund our effort. Each dealership would put up the money to sponsor one bike powered by overbored Triumph twins, which Eric would build into one of his tried and tested motocross frames. I got the motors straight from the production line at Meriden and stripped, balanced and rebuilt them. As with all of my previous bikes, I changed the gearing to include a low first and then a jump to the close-ratio other three gears, which gave a top speed of around 100mph on the road. They weren't quite as smooth as my previous factory bikes, but really came into their own on the motocross track which was used on a daily basis to decide evaluation points."

The event, centred on the small Spanish town of El Escorial, didn't start well for the British team when on day one they lost 21 marks after John Pease was plagued by punctures and then John Giles suffered a split petrol tank. To counter this problem, recurring instructions were given for the rest of the team to ride with their spare gloves stuffed under the tanks, which worked a treat. No more marks were lost, and at the end the British team finished a heady sixth with the trio of Jim Sandiford, Mick Wilkinson and team captain Ken leading the over half-litre class and beating the much fancied West German BMW-mounted team in the process.

For 1971 the ISDT returned to the Isle of Man; for Ken, who was selected as both rider and team manager, this was his swansong, and he signed off with the last of his gold medals. Combining the duties of both rider and team manager was not easy, and Ken is quick to acknowledge the huge amount of help he received from his right-hand men Chris Oliver and Ian Driver, and the support teams made up of volunteers from the Met police and the REME at Bordon.

The present owner of Ken's old Cheney WCG 101H, Alan Davey, was in the IOM as a spectator, and when he knew Ken was retiring he bought it for the princely sum of £425 on the 18th of December 1971. A very nice early Christmas present if ever there was! Alan rode it in the Welsh for three years picking up bronze medals for his efforts, and also in a couple of Lands End trials, but he has managed to keep it in remarkably original condition.

Looking over the bike, it bristles with the former owner's neat and thoughtful detail touches, which include a metre of spare oil pipe inside the handlebars, replacement coils, QD wheels, a hook on top of the guard to hold the chain, spare cables strapped in position, and a throttle cable which could be changed in a matter of seconds.

The ability to change items quickly was the difference between winning and losing a gold medal, and the throttle cable is a typical example of Ken's ingenuity and preparation.

"99 per cent of throttle cable breakages happen at the twist grip, so to have this easily accessible I cut a groove in the twist grip assembly and covered it with plastic tape. I then made up a short length of cable which went into a splitter box, so in the event of a breakage I could change it in about twenty seconds without touching the carburettor or even dismounting."

After thirty years at the top flight, 1972 also saw Ken's retirement from scrambling, and he entered a new stage of his ISDT career when he was appointed British team manager. For the next three years the same meticulous approach which had seen him achieve so much success as a rider was put into a plethora of activities which ranged from selecting the team and negotiating with sponsors to organising the support crews. This approach to planning was exemplified in 1974, when along with Peter Howdle and Alan Kimber, Ken rode a 650cc police specification Triumph Thunderbird to the Abruzzi mountains in southern Italy to reconnoitre the route and walk the hills a month before the event.

KEN HEANES - MR ISDT

In addition to all of this and running his four motorcycle shops, he also found time to manage the Maudes trophy-winning BMW team in the Isle of Man and a Suzuki record attempt at Monza, where he earned the nickname of 'Horizontal'. The latter was given because of his ability to fall asleep on the pit wall between changing riders and tyres for the successful Suzuki team, which included Ernst Degner, Stuart Graham and Tommy Robb in its line-up.

Ken was undoubtedly both a successful rider and businessman, but above all he was extremely well liked and respected, especially amongst his loyal staff who knew him as 'a good guvn'r'.

Although retired from the motorcycle trade for the last 18 years there is usually a project or two going on in his workshop, and an immaculately restored Triumph Tiger 100 often takes him to the village post office to collect his pension. I had a great day talking to Ken, and it is a privilege to be able to commit some of the good old days of the ISDT to print.

ISDT Cheney Triumphs bikes and riders

1970 Spain
WCG 101H .. .. Ken Heanes
WCG 102H .. .. Jim Sandiford
WCG 103H .. .. Malcolm Rathmell
WCG 104H .. .. John Giles
WCG 105H .. .. Mick Wilkinson
WCG 106H .. .. John Pease
WCG 112H .. .. Colin Dommett (Reserve)

1971 Isle of Man
WCG 101H .. .. Ken Heanes
WCG 102H .. .. Jim Sandiford
WCG 103H .. .. Malcolm Rathmell
WCG 104H .. .. Mick Andrews
WCG 105H .. .. Mick Wilkinson
WCG 106H .. .. John Pease
WCG 112H .. .. Arthur Browning (Reserve)

Wonderful action shot as Ken aviates the Triumph Metisse at a Weymouth scramble in April 1963.

Max on the bike that changed trials – testing Sammy Miller's first Bultaco in 1965.

CHAPTER 15
MAX KING

When Max King started trial riding in the years after WW2, he was lucky in that he had a mentor close at hand. However, if an aspiring rider didn't have any such guidance close by, what was he to do? Max decided to take action.

It's a wet and muddy West of England trial in 1958, and struggling to keep his works Francis Barnett moving over the slippery granite slabs is local man Max King.

In front of a gallery of spectators King is footing strongly, when fellow competitor Ivan Pridham is heard to yell "Read page 34, Max."

The good-natured banter was a reference to Max's best-selling book *Trials Riding*, and it was a jibe which the author would have to endure many times during his career. Not only would its content inspire many a mud-plugger to take up the sport, it would also make Max King as well-known as contemporary aces Viney, Miller and Jackson. In fact, such was its popularity the first edition – printed in 1955 – sold a staggering 20,000 copies. Hitherto there had been nothing available to give that much-needed guidance on which bike to buy, what to wear and how to negotiate different types of section – so to learn that it sold well is perhaps not surprising.

Although aimed primarily at the novice rider it held wide appeal, and some years later – on its second reprint – works Greeves ace Don Smith told Max (rather tongue in cheek, mind you) that he "always had a well-thumbed copy strapped to the tank of his bike!"

However, as he legged out of that section in the West of England, Max only had time for a rueful smile – dusk had set in, the clock was ticking and, as he was due in Exeter at 6.15pm, there would be no opportunity for post-trial socialising.

To find out more about this dash to Exeter, the famous book and his long trials riding career, I visited Max at his home in north Devon. So why, I asked, was he in such a rush that day to finish and get away from the trial?

"When my book came out, the publisher, Temple Press, sent copies to all sorts of potential reviewers including the BBC. I was working in my job at County Hall in Dorchester when I received a phone call from my wife, Peggy. She told me there was a letter at home from the BBC, so, intrigued as to its content, I asked her to open it. It was from Peter Lord, the then sports producer in Bristol, who, it transpired, was looking for a Saturday afternoon motoring correspondent. He'd read my book and thought I might be suitable for the role, so if interested 'could I please arrange to go to the studio for an audition the following Saturday?'

'You will won't you?' asked Peggy, so I decided I'd better phone him and find out what he had in mind.

Max negotiating a muddy stream on the works Francis Barnett at an Otter Vale trial in October 1962.

On the 250cc BSA, Max keeps his feet up in a 1960 trial at Sturminster Newton.

"I TOLD MY MOTHER THAT WHEN I WAS OLDER THIS WAS WHAT I WANTED TO DO, BUT SHE INSTANTLY POURED COLD WATER ON THE IDEA"

Off-Road Giants!

Another clean on the 250cc BSA – location unknown.

'Prepare a script of two minutes' duration – no more, no less – of a trial that you've witnessed, and come to the studio on Saturday morning.'

I duly arrived to what seemed to me like chaos, with people rushing about all over the place, but eventually I met Peter Lord and we went into the studio where I was to be auditioned."

At that juncture in his day job, Max – who was later to rise to become divisional director with Wessex Water – was Dorset's public health engineer, so was well versed and equipped for reading reports. However, as he soon discovered, delivering a radio news report called for a very different technique to that which he was used to.

"I finished bang on two minutes, and in my headphones Peter Lord said 'that was bloody awful, you're not reading a report for a committee, imagine that you're just chatting to me and make it more newsey.' I went into a quiet corner and rewrote it – I was a fairly formal sort of chap, so I changed things like 'I have' and 'do not' to 'I've' and 'don't' and after a couple of retakes it sounded quite reasonable. Peter asked me when the next event was and I told him it was the following Saturday's West of England trial in which I was riding. He told me that after the trial I was to report to the Exeter police station where I would collect the key to the nearby – unmanned – BBC studio. I would then 'Take the lift to the third floor, turn on the main switch, put on the headphones and listen for the presenter, who will cue you in from the Bristol studio with the words 'To report on today's West of England motorcycle trial here's Max King,' and you'll speak for two minutes – the same duration as reports on other sports.'

After heavy overnight rain the trial itself was very muddy resulting in quite a lot of hold-ups and delays; after I finished and signed off I had time to drive to a lay-by and write my 'two minute' script before journeying on to Heavitree police station.

I'd rather assumed that collecting the key would be a straightforward affair; however, I got there to discover a queue of people reporting all sorts of losses and problems. On top of that there was a sergeant who obviously wasn't going to be rushed and I was starting to get very anxious. I told him that I just needed the BBC studio key but he replied in a slow voice 'just take your time sir.' I eventually got the key, let myself in, turned on the switch and put on the headphones. As I pulled them over my ears I heard the producer's voice frantically saying 'Where the hell have you been?' There was little or no time to give my excuses so I awaited my cue and gave my report. I suppose it was ok, because I carried on broadcasting on *Sports Page* for the next twenty odd years!"

We'll be returning for more radio and TV tales later, but firstly lets backtrack to the 1920s, with Max telling me how he first became interested in motorcycles.

"As a young lad I'd read comics like *The Champion* (and *Billy Bunter*) but when I was about ten my mother brought home a copy of *The Modern Boy* story paper. There were several articles about cars and motorbikes, and I vividly recall one on a new Rex Acme which I found absolutely fascinating! A friend of my father owned a 250 Excelsior JAP, and he further fuelled my interest with an Easter Saturday pillion ride to Barbrook, near Lynton. We arrived just as it was getting light to watch competitors in the Land's End trial tackle the renowned Beggar's Roost. I think it must have been about 1927, and I can recall that I was very excited and particularly keen to see how our local man, Bill Bray on his New Imperial, would fare on 'The Roost'. Sadly, he attacked it much too slowly and fell off in a big heap."

It would be another twenty-three years before Max would also be riding in the Land's End, although, as he told me, his announcement that he wanted to ride in motorcycle trials didn't meet with much parental enthusiasm.

"I told my mother that when I was older this was what I wanted to do, but she instantly poured cold water on the idea. She told me that motorbikes were dangerous and 'a young boy like you should get properly educated and professionally qualified. Those are the things to concentrate on, not motorcycle trials.'"

Max's protestations that trials were safe and didn't need the daredevil use of speed fell on deaf ears – although it would seem that riding on the road was deemed much safer, for in 1932 he got his first machine, a brand-new 250 OHV BSA, and later a 246 Sunbeam.

"I'd become an articled pupil to a public health engineer in Barnstaple; I qualified in public health in 1937 and in March 1939 was appointed public health engineer to Bideford RDC. But in September war started, and in July 1940 I joined the RAF. I was demobbed in September 1945; by then I was married and had a young son. So I had a family home to set up and still had to qualify as a civil engineer, but I remained as keen as ever to try my hand at trials."

Max's wish would become reality when in February 1949, at the

In his Saturday morning job, Max tests the latest 250cc Greeves in 1964.

"I RODE THE BIKE TO THE TRIAL AND CAN STILL VIVIDLY RECALL THE SECOND SECTION ... IT FEATURED AN ICE-BOUND GRADIENT MADE UP LARGELY OF FROZEN COW DUNG"

Off-Road Giants!

age of thirty-three, he entered his first event, the West of England club's Knill trial starting at Ashburton.

"Shortly after Peggy and I had moved to Exeter, I happened to see one of our neighbours riding a B32 trials bike into and out of a stream with steep banks interspersed with saplings. It was only a hundred yards away; he seemed pretty good, I got talking to him and found out his name was Ken Haydon (his son Ian would later ride for Montesa). I told Ken that I'd long fancied having a go at trials and had already bought a nearly new alloy-barrelled 350 AJS. Ken – who later became a good friend – told me that when I was ready he'd teach me to ride."

The first training session took place at the aptly named Scratchy Face Lane, and a few weeks later Max entered his first event – that infamous Knill trial! But as he struggled around the frozen 80 mile course he began to question his wisdom!

"I rode the bike to the trial and can still vividly recall the second section; it was called Cuming and featured an ice-bound gradient made up largely of frozen cow dung. I was so cold that I decided there and then that I would never do another trial, yet, come what may, I was going to make it to the finish. If I remember correctly, Ariel man Bob Ray lost eighteen marks and beat runner-up Nipper Parsons by one. I managed to make it to the end, but lost the best part of ninety in the process."

Later that year Max changed to a 500 Matchless, and in May 1949 won his first award, the novice cup, in the Exmoor club's OTC trial – an event in which two years later he showed how much he'd improved by beating his mentor Haydon to take the class award on a 197 Francis Barnett.

1950 saw the start of a happy association with the MCC long distance trials, and aboard a 500 Triumph Trophy, the line-up of King, Bill Kershaw and Ken Hooper – also on TR5s – took the much-prized one make team award in the Land's End. The TR5 – which also doubled up for occasional road use – was ideally suited to the long distance events, and would carry Max to several more MCC golds, but in one day trials he'd given up on 'big bangers', and by '52 was on a 197 Francis Barnett. On the little stroker he was starting to get himself noticed, and added to his burgeoning collection of silverware with class wins and a number of 1st and 2nd class awards. He won his first premier in the Meech Cup trial in 1953, and repeated this success in 1956. A big scalp for Max was that of AMC works rider and friend Bill Martin, to win Otter Vale's Pop's Trophy trial by two marks!

In Ken Haydon, Max had an excellent mentor, but as he'd discovered there was little or no written information available on how to start or what to do. What was needed was a book, and during the winter of '53/'54 one took shape; although as he typed away in the family kitchen little could the author have imagined the success it would be.

"Peggy and I had moved to Dorchester, and the manuscript was written on a portable typewriter in the kitchen of our temporary home in Queens Avenue while our new house was being built. Working two hours a night it took a winter to complete, but then of course I had to try to get it published. After initially trying Pitman's it was suggested I contact Temple Press, which was then publisher of *Motorcycling*, or the *Green 'un*. It showed interest, but would only consider publishing it if I could get a champion rider to write the foreword. They asked me who was then the best rider and naturally I said Hugh Viney. They then asked if I knew him personally – I said that I did, but not well. The motorcycle show was coming up so on the Monday, with brief case in hand, I went to Earl's Court in the vain hope that I might see him. Celebrities were often elusive around the main public areas, yet who should be on the AJS stand but the man himself, Hugh Viney. I had to remind him who I was, but after a bit of small talk ventured to tell him that I'd written a book on trials riding and asked if he would consider writing the foreword.

'Depends how good it is,' said Viney. With that I produced the manuscript from the brief case and told him I would return on the Thursday, if convenient, for his frank opinion. Hugh was usually a rather dour looking chap, but when I returned three days later he had a smile on his face and said 'I think it's splendid, I've already written some words for the foreword but please alter it as you see fit.'"

The rest, as they say, is history. *Trials Riding* would later go on to be enlarged, and renamed *Motor Cycle Trials Riding* by Pelhams, the new publishers. There was a version in Spanish, and in all there were five reprints, with Mick Andrews, Gordon Farley and Malcolm Rathmell all adding their names to that of Hugh Viney by way of forewords.

Max rode Francis Barnetts until 1959, when he changed to a 4-stroke BSA C15T YOE 388. This bike was a standard C15T but was later modified by the factory. In 1964 – with Brian Martin's approval – it was loaned to Vic Ashford, who rode it to equal first in the south west centre championship.

Speaking of his Saturday slot on *Sports Page*, Max told me that this had become very popular and Tony Smith – who had then taken over as sports producer – had asked if he could report on more of the Saturday nationals. Max told the producer that as much as he would like to do this, it simply wasn't feasible. "I have a highly responsible and demanding professional job, but what I could do is ask my good friend Ralph Venables MBE, a world class journalist, to help out. Ralph attends all the national trials and I feel sure that an arrangement could be made for him to phone me in the studio with the highlights in typically graphic style.

Ralph readily agreed and for many years this format worked a treat. At the end of the trial he would find the nearest phone box, reverse charges and talk to me long enough to tell what I needed – often these conversations lasted 30 minutes or more. I was then able to prepare my script; sometimes, in the producer's opinion, with more colour than if I had been there myself!

Motorcycle News started in 1955, and soon after a sub-editor contacted me asking if I would report on selected events in the south and assist in reporting the Scottish six days for it."

It would be the start of a long association between Max and *MCN*. The 'Scottish' also opened another broadcasting door.

"I was surprised to learn through the BBC that up until that time – the late '50s – there was little or no radio coverage of the Scottish, so I got in touch with Murdoch McPherson, the then BBC Radio Scotland sports producer. He agreed to me broadcasting twice daily reports during the trial to Radio Highland and, as required, to Radio Scotland. These six days bulletins were very well received, and what started as a one off broadcast continued annually for about twenty years."

Max's journalistic activities went on in his own time, in tandem with his very demanding job in the water industry.

"*MCN* saw me as a useful chap to have around. But to cover two, sometimes three events over a weekend and meet the deadlines on

Max puts the works 250cc Cotton through its paces.

Sunday evenings was, as you can imagine, sometimes rather fraught. The book had sold well in America, and this backed up by my work for MCN brought an invitation from one of the leading stateside magazines, *Cycle World*. It was keen to read about events like the Scottish six days, and I also did a piece on the burgeoning sport of schoolboy scrambling featuring the Jennings family from Bristol. Also for MCN, I did appraisals of new trials bikes, and thanks to Sammy Miller, in May 1965 I got to test-ride the first production Bultaco in the UK. It was a revelation, and my test report praised it accordingly – such that there was a clamour to change machines in time for north Devon MC's Whitsuntide President's Cup trial.

The appraisal format was that Gordon Francis and I would go out on a Saturday morning to the testing ground, and while I did the riding Gordon took his shots. Over the years I tested many bikes. It was a fascinating job, and perhaps the most interesting was Sammy's prototype works 250 Honda SAM 1N.

In the mid-sixties competition was losing its appeal, and I recall a wet, muddy day in an Otter Vale trial, on Harold Ellis' farm at Exwick, waiting in a queue with chaps half my age. I asked myself 'Why am I here? I've achieved what I wanted to do.' Soon after I decided to call it a day."

Although Max retired from one day trials he continued to compete in his much loved MCC classics, and in 1970 accomplished the rare – possibly unique – distinction of winning a Triple on a combination of two and four wheels. A Triple is awarded for winning gold or higher in the Exeter, Land's End and Edinburgh in the same MCC trials year; in 1970 Max – driving a Hartwell (Sunbeam) Imp – won his class in the Exeter and Land's End, but the Imp was not available for the Edinburgh. With the approval of the organisers, Max rode a bike – Ken Heanes' ex-ISDT Triumph – and he duly won gold; this despite a broken clutch cable in the middle of the night which threatened to scupper his chances.

If you remember the TV programme *Kickstart*, then you might recall that it was Max who appeared alongside the exuberant Dave Lee Travis in the first series as technical commentator; a job that came about in a roundabout way.

"I did most of the media work for Wessex Water while I was with them, so when the TV wanted an interview it was to me that the publicity manager turned. During the drought of '76, especially, I was virtually on call 24 hours a day. Although I didn't realise it at the time, it later opened an avenue to doing a bit of work on television. The BBC had come to interview me regarding a water problem and in an off-camera conversation with the producer I mentioned my motorcycle sport involvement for BBC radio. The producer said 'I'll bear that in mind' and some time later, after my retirement from Wessex, he phoned me with an invitation to join the team for the newly planned TV trials programme *Kickstart*. It was certainly highly enjoyable."

Undoubtedly what came across powerfully to the armchair viewer was Max's huge appetite and enthusiasm for motorcycle sport – an enthusiasm which in his ninetieth year is still as strong as that day in 1927 when the young, excited King went to Beggar's Roost on the 250 Excelsior JAP, or on that fateful Monday in 1955 and the chance encounter with Hugh Viney.

One of Mike's early 250cc motocross GPs on his newly-acquired Greeves in 1958.

Mike Jackson went on to a career in the motorcycle industry, but in his earlier days on factory-supported Francis Barnetts and Greeves he was a keen and successful off-road competitor, both at home and abroad.

CHAPTER 16
MIKE JACKSON

Old MJ's competition years

It's 1958, and, armed with a new 197cc Greeves Hawkestone, a young Mike Jackson is readying both himself and machine for the following weekend's Belgian MXGP at Namur. Fuelled with the confidence of youth, the running-in process is limited to a few smokey laps of the family's Southampton garden before the budding GP star is satisfied that all is well – the engine dies, the trail of 2-stroke smoke disperses, and peace is once again restored to the quiet suburbs.

History would record that he would be rewarded with a well-deserved 10th overall in that race, but more importantly it would herald the start of an enduring relationship between Mike and the Greeves factory which would last until nearly the end of the following decade.

Nowadays of course, 'Old MJ' is a familiar sight around the classic bike scene, and after a lifetime's involvement with motorcycling is still an extremely busy man. Many of us will have read his well-penned articles of the years spent with Norton and NVT during the period 1969-1982, so it probably comes as no surprise to learn that he is a journalist of long standing; a job which started as an unpaid contributor to the *Southern Centre Gazette* back in the mid-sixties. Naturally eloquent, this makes him the perfect choice as chairman and organiser of the popular Friends Off-Road Evenings at Beaulieu, which he's made very much his own and for which he is now probably best known. With such a plethora of jobs and roles it's all too easy to overlook that of Mike Jackson, competition rider, one that I first witnessed at a windy Beenham Park in October 1962.

It was a day which saw some of the country's best 250cc riders line up for battle in the two-leg lightweight championship, including the debut of Vic Eastwood on the works James and one Mike Jackson on a Greeves. Recent referral to my programme of the event revealed that by virtue of his win in the second leg, Mike's fellow Greeves rider Joe Johnson emerged overall victor after turning the tables on Don Rickman, who was first past the flag in leg one on the Bultaco Metisse; a report in a faded press cutting providing a fitting reminder of some fantastically close racing. The results also revealed that after a promising ride in the first leg in which he finished sixth, Eastwood was out of the points in the second, and Mike – who by then was a fully fledged member of the Thundersley fold – had a disappointing day, finishing 11th and 8th.

A rare bad day for the man from Southampton, but as the decade progressed the liaison, which started for Mike and Greeves on that day

One of Mike's last races on the works Francis Barnett at the French GP at Cassel in 1958.

"WITH SUCH A PLETHORA OF JOBS AND ROLES IT'S ALL TOO EASY TO OVERLOOK THAT OF MIKE JACKSON, COMPETITION RIDER"

Typical scrambles action sees Mike dicing with fellow Greeves rider Roger Snoad. (Photo Mike Jackson archive)

Off-Road Giants!

In trials action on the 250cc Greeves in the Perce Simon event in the New Forest. (Photo Mike Jackson archive)

have possessed the in-depth 2-stroke technical know-how of 'Herman the German', but he was extremely thorough in the way he assembled the engines and his whole machine preparation was second to none. After all, it's no good having a more powerful engine if the wheel spindle is bent or the brakes are binding. Immaculate presentation and preparation were the hallmarks of any Sharp bike, and if you spun the wheel it would always revolve a little bit longer than anyone else's.

I loved France from various family holidays and longed to ride there, especially as I'd heard tales from fellow riders about the motocross which – along with the birds and the wine – created a wonderful atmosphere and ambience, so I set about doing a lot of the national opens to get some good results to qualify. If you won a 250cc national you'd qualify straight away, but frankly I wasn't going to beat the likes of John Clayton and Triss Sharp – but I got a few thirds, fourths and fifths.

I was then aged 18, and decided to invite Sam Huggett [the ACU's all-powerful secretary] out to lunch, which was a bit cheeky I guess. This was in the autumn of 1957, and we went out to a posh restaurant and I said 'I may not have earned enough points, but I'll behave myself, and could I do up to a maximum of four holiday rides? I promise I won't let you down and I am trying to get some points anyway in the nationals.' I think I actually did get enough points but he gave his permission to ride up to the maximum of four and I also lobbied Harold Taylor, who met me and said 'You wrote an intelligent letter laddie, and you seem to be a decent rider, you won't let the side down!'"

The ACU was undoubtedly keen to ensure that British riders were both competitive and would behave themselves while representing the ACU on the continent; however, as Mike was to find out, despite being granted permission to ride, the actual obtaining of entries proved slightly more difficult, especially in the smaller meetings. Therefore his continental debut came about in the 1958 French GP, which he told me about.

in 1958, would reap many rewards. I met Mike at his favourite local near Salisbury where we relived some of those halcyon days, and I started by asking him what led to that first Greeves ride and how his off-road career began.

"By 1956 I'd graduated to riding an ex-Sharp 197cc Francis Barnett, and thanks to the way it had been prepared by 'Pop' Sharp it really flew. This enabled me to win the southern centre scrambles championship for the next three years. In those days a standard Barnett in scrambles trim was turning out about 9.5bhp and 2-stroke tuning was looked upon as very much a black art. Very few of the so-called experts had a clue what they were doing, and after being 'race prepared' the power output often dropped to as little as 6bhp with the only increase being in the noise it made, but Pops was very different. He may not

"In those days the 250 and 500cc GPs were on the same day on the same course. This changed in '59, but I wrote off to the Grand Prix organisers pretty much as a last resort, and surprisingly had quite good responses and start money offers. For my first ever event in May '58 I went with Gordon Francis along with the Barnett – which by then had grown to 225cc and featured BSA front forks – to the French GP at Mont Cassel in my A50 pick-up truck. It rained hard which gave the muddy conditions that usually suited me, but I was unable to capitalise on it and finished a fairly dismal 14th in a race won by Jaromir Cizek

On the works Greeves at a TV scramble at Old Park, Beaulieu.

Negotiating the thick Tanner Trudge mud in 1962 on his Greeves, in an event that he won.

Off-Road Giants!

on the works Jawa. If I recall correctly I got paid about thirty-five quid, which covered my ferry crossing from Dover to Bolougne, food, petrol and a couple of nights bed and breakfast. It wasn't riches, but what it did mean was that I got to watch the 500cc world championship race for free, and what racing it was. John Draper – who was one of my great heroes – was in scintillating form that day, and lapped everyone up to fourth place including Bill Nilsson, who had won the championship the previous year – although out of courtesy he let Bill un-lap himself on the final circuit. I've got a feeling it was also Gordon Francis' first continental GP, and he took a wonderful photograph of the British contingent celebrating with the victorious Draper wrapped in the union flag. 'Drapes' was a great character, and while everyone else was doing their best just to stay on he rode along the muddy start/finish straight larking about and making gestures with his arms as if he was driving a tractor!"

In the same year Mike also rode in both the Dutch and Belgian races, but he was getting a little disenchanted with the Barnetts, and as he told me a frame breakage in Italy heralded the change to Greeves.

"By now the Barnett had a full 250cc AMC engine which I was told was the bee's knees, and although the Norton forks made it handle better the engine didn't turn out any more power than the old 197. In fact, the heavier engine obviated any advantage gained through handling, and I was not really making any progress on it. It was a long drive to Italy and if I recall I was the only British rider there, so as you can imagine I wasn't particularly pleased when the frame snapped in the first moto. Fed up, I drove back to the UK overnight, red-eye style, and was on the forecourt at the Thundersley factory by Tuesday morning. I collected a new Hawkestone which I rode around the garden on the Wednesday, and by the Friday it was loaded on the A50 and off to Belgium for the GP. I paid retail price for the bike through Pop Sharp, who had by then opened a shop in Bournemouth, although Derry Preston-Cobb said that he would monitor my progress, and depending on how I got on would help me with some 'good prices' on spares in the future."

We'll be covering some more of Mike's years with Greeves later, but it's all to easy to lose sight of the fact that he was also a top class southern centre trials rider, and it was in the feet up game that he started his off-road career in 1954. I asked him about the lead-up to that debut trial.

"My father ran a family building and property firm in Southampton and had no interest in motorcycling, but my brother – who was five years my senior – started riding in trials at sixteen. In those days there were no schoolboy events, so I had to wait five frustrating years before I too could ride."

For the young Mike boarding school soon followed, but with the weekly delivery of the motorcycle press to look forward to there was no shortage in his diet of motorcycling, and a seventeen-mile cycle ride to Draper's Farm held much more appeal than cricket.

"As soon as my brother started riding I became addicted to the reports in the *Blue 'un* and *Green 'un*, so I knew exactly where all the major scrambles and trials were held. It was decided that it was time for me to go to boarding school, so my father – who was an eccentric vegetarian – located two such schools, one in Hertfordshire and the other at Stonehouse in Gloucestershire. At twelve years old he gave me the choice of which one to go to, and as there was all this motorcycling going on in and around Stroud including the Cotswold Cup trial held only three miles away from the school, you can imagine it didn't take too long to make my decision. I don't know how but I managed to get a dispensation to miss cricket, and I would cycle over to Draper's Farm at Prestbury to watch the scrambles, and would also ride down many of the Cotswold trial sections on my bicycle, which taught me a lot about balance and braking control.

Just after my sixteenth birthday in August 1954, I made my trials debut in the Blackmore Vale Alan cup event on my brother's rigid James Commando, this pending the arrival of a rigid 197cc Norman.

Mike admits he wasn't a naturally gifted rider, but there was no lack of enthusiasm. Nine months later in May 1955 he lined up for his first scramble.

"I'd been trialling all winter, and ahead of my first scramble had been practising on the building sites which left the poor old Norman absolutely worn out, so I'd replaced it with a second-hand Commando from Sid Lawton. I decided that it needed a swinging arm and we took it to Len Harfield for one of his conversions, but by May it wasn't ready, so I used my brother's 500cc Triumph Trophy and surprisingly came away from my first event at West Wellow with 7/6d in prize money."

After a season riding in trials and practising on the quagmire conditions of building sites Mike became adept at riding on mud, although he was ill-prepared for his second scramble at Bulbarrow Hill.

"The Len Harfield spring conversion had been carried out and I lined up feeling pretty confident, but no one had told me about putting 'knobblies' on the bike. The track at Pinns Farm was lush and boggy meadow so there were no high speeds, and several of us rode on trials tyres with no real problems. I didn't appreciate the huge difference in grip between the two, and despite all my best efforts I couldn't get up the steepest climb at Bulbarrow and fell off. Sadly I slipped back down the hill right into the path of Ivor England, who was getting grip-a-plenty from the knobblies on his 197cc Dot, including some from my ankle which he rode over and broke."

Amazingly, within a month Mike was riding again and was immediately upgraded to Expert status, which he told me about.

"The first meeting after breaking my leg was incredibly muddy, and with the Harfield James now sporting knobblies I managed to win every race. I was still a novice but in those days you were upgraded immediately, so I came away from the meeting at the Pinns Farm 'mud derby' with £7 in prize money, which was ok, and now as an Expert, which was intimidating! This was rather harsh, as after only three meetings I was suddenly pitched in with a bunch of very experienced riders on 500s so the rest of the season was a struggle."

And it wasn't just against the opposition that Mike was struggling – the bike seemed to be getting progressively slower with each meeting.

"No one had mentioned the importance of changing piston rings or oil seals, and while the Sharp brothers' bikes went progressively faster mine was slug-like in comparison. All it needed was a decent engine, and that came about after my brother approached Triss Senior with a polite request to rebuild the 8E to bog-standard specification. As with all of his bikes it only turned out about 9.5bhp, but at least I was able to get on the pace and be competitive."

With the connection now in place the Jackson brothers bought two ex-Sharp Francis Barnetts, whereafter Mike would soon win his first southern centre scrambles star, although at trials he was very

Leading the South Down Experts on the Greeves Challenger in 1966.

Off-Road Giants!

much in the doldrums. He'd achieved Expert status, but on his own admission never fully got to grips with the green Francis Barnett trials bike, and although he picked up the odd first class award it would be two more years before he was back to his best. This would be the start of the association with Greeves, and in his first trials season in 1958 Mike and the new 197cc Scottish became a formidable combination in the southern centre mud. With the lessons learned well from those lengthy building site practice sessions, he became a master of gooey and glutinous going; although as he told me, he was not quite so adept when it came to rocks.

"In scrambles I had no problems racing across stony going, but in trials I must have been the worst rider on rocks of anyone in the UK. I tried all I knew but was absolutely useless, and as a result received a lot of good-natured banter from Peter Gaunt who gave me the nickname of SP ('southern ponce'). I rode in some of the nationals but didn't ever compete in Scotland for the six days as I had the perfect excuse that it clashed with the scrambles season!"

Mike took to the Greeves like a duck to water, but by '59 all of the full works riders were on full blown 250s, and like many of his contemporaries he started to explore ways of making up for this power deficiency. One of the favourite 'big bores' came courtesy of Vale-Onslow, and as Mike explained they proved to be fast but frail.

"The Vale Onslow conversion immediately gave the Villiers engine a 30 per cent increase in power and it would go like stink for a while, but sadly the pistons were poor quality and would disintegrate with some pretty catastrophic results. I bought one of the conversions and left it with Pop Sharp, who promptly contacted Hepolite which made a one-off batch of pistons for £6 each. The only other modification was to the jetting, and the engine ran faultlessly for over two seasons with perfect reliability."

From the time he left school Mike's 'day job' had been to assist with the family's building firm, but by '63 he was feeling fed up with bricks and mortar and the perfect opening came when he heard Mr Sharp was retiring as Greeves' South of England representative.

"He'd sold his shop and had been repping throughout the south west for Greeves, although it was all done on a very casual sort of basis with no set round, but he was extremely popular. I think they had 44 applicants for the job which covered an area from Kent to Cornwall and paid £7 10s per week, plus a small commission on the sale of bikes and 3d a mile for petrol. To my surprise I got the job, but both Mr Greeves and Derry Preston-Cobb had reservations about taking me on as they thought that I was a bit of a playboy, and Cobby said 'Mike, I'm keeping my fingers crossed on my good hand that you'll be ok.' I started on January 1st 1964 and by 11.00am had my first two orders for a couple of trials bikes from Bob Gollner, and on the second day managed to get a dealer to pay us a long outstanding £17 spares invoice which instantly got me into the good books of our accounts dept."

For the next five years Mike continued to both ride and sell the Thundersley bikes, but was continually frustrated by the fact that it couldn't produce enough to satisfy demand. This was particularly true for the potentially lucrative stateside market, and in '68 he put a proposal to Preston-Cobb that he (Mike) should make a fact-finding trip to the USA.

"I asked Cobby to pay me a working wage to include some accommodation and mileage allowance and I would go around to every one of Nicholson's (Greeves California importer) dealers. I proposed that I would buy two bikes and take them on my car and trailer which would be shipped on the Queen Mary and do a three month whistle-stop tour of the USA, including some demo and publicity rides. Cobby thought that it was a fantastic idea, but had to put it to Mr Greeves who not only turned it down flat, but steadfastly refused any discussion on the subject."

Bert Greeves' rejection heralded the end for Mike, and despite offers of a pay rise and possible directorship, by the following April he was looking around for another job.

Mike Jackson: life as a mover and shaker

It's February 1972, Long Beach California, and Norton's 'man in America' is on his way to the preview of *On Any Sunday*, a semi-documentary movie starring one of Hollywood's hottest properties, Steve McQueen.

Mike, who three years earlier had been flogging a Kent to Cornwall sales patch as Greeves' southern representative, was now moving in famous circles. As he journeyed to the film preview that night he carried in his pocket a fax from his boss in England, Dennis Poore, saying "Approach McQueen and, for the right consideration, enquire if he's willing to feature on next year's Norton poster."

Following Bert Greeves steadfast refusal to allow Mike to go to the states – or even to discuss his reasons why not – he'd looked around for another job, and was quickly appointed by Norton Villiers as its European sales manager.

With the demise of AMC, AJS had been taken over by Norton Villiers which – acutely aware of the marque's former competition successes – had revived the name with its new Y4 Stormer scrambler. Old timers might have scoffed at the notion that a ring dinging 2-stroke should carry the once famous name, but in the hands of Andy Roberton and Malcolm Davis there was no denying the machine's potential. There were wins for the duo in the Grandstand and World of Sport TV scrambles, and in addition Davies scooped the 250cc British championship.

The spin-offs were obvious, so AJS advertised for a European sales manager, a position ideal for Mike – although, as he told me, one he thought had eluded him.

"I applied for the job and went for an interview held in a portacabin which was then the AJS 'office' in January 1969. They had over 40 applicants, many of whom I considered were far better qualified for the position, so when I hadn't heard anything by April I assumed that they had appointed someone else."

Amidst a fanfare of publicity the new 750cc Honda was being launched at a motorcycle show in Brighton's Metropole exhibition centre, attended by Mike as the Greeves representative; although as he was about to discover, his time with the Thundersley firm would shortly conclude.

"I was at the show when Norton's John McDermott sidled up, and whispered, 'You've got the job, can you start on Monday?'

It was pretty obvious that I couldn't do that, as firstly I had to disentangle myself from my position at Greeves and also tender my resignation, something which as I told McDermott I wanted to do in person."

112

Mike in America with his 1970 Chevrolet Camaro – it had a 4.5-litre V8 engine and he could fill the 22US gallon tank for £3 in the early seventies. (Photo Mike Jackson archive)

"MIKE HAD MADE HIS
MIND UP, AND DESPITE
OFFERS OF A PAY RISE AND
A POSSIBLE DIRECTORSHIP

Off-Road Giants!

It would be two more weeks before Jackson could get a meeting with Derry Preston Cobb, who was understandably disappointed with his decision. However, Mike had made his mind up, and despite offers of a pay rise and a possible directorship was on his way to AJS – although unusually, he didn't actually start on a Monday.

"I'd been selected to ask a question as a member of the audience for *Does the team think?*, a radio show which starred amongst others Ted Ray and Jimmy Edwards. An added attraction was that the BBC paid the princely sum of £3 17s 6d to attendees, therefore because of 'a busy prior engagement' I started with AJS on a Tuesday, my job specification a simple one; 'get out and sell these bikes!'"

Mike was a born salesman and soon the order books were brimming full, especially from enthusiastic off-road dealerships like Fowlers and Comerfords.

Although AJS lost the brilliant Davis to CZ, Roberton was later joined by a plethora of top stars including Vic Eastwood, Chris Horsfield and Roger Harvey, all of whom rode the 250, 370, and later 410cc bikes with a great deal of success. And if they needed a bit of extra publicity, then a young road-racer called Barry Sheene was quite happy to come along for a photo shoot and test the bike. As Mike recalled, this was in the days before he (Sheene) became famous, and it cost AJS just £15 plus a ploughman's lunch for Bazza and 'bird' at the local pub!

Not only did Mike sell AJS, he was still racing and winning on them – although by June 1970 he'd swapped the quagmire conditions of Farleigh castle for the Californian desert; a move which, as he revealed probably, had a helping hand from one of Norton's directors.

"I did what I thought was a bit of sales 'whiz kiddery' and as a result upset Norton sales director, Philip Sellars. At that time it was just starting its own distribution outlet in America, which went under the name of NVC (Norton/Villiers Corporation). 90 per cent of sales were Norton road bikes while the other 10 per cent was AJS. They'd previously had two sales managers, one Brit and one American, but for various reasons neither had been particularly suitable, so Sellars suggested to Dennis Poore 'Mike Jackson's very good, why don't you send him out there?'"

Whether this was a ploy to 'bury' Mike is unclear, but on June 15th 1970, and only a year after joining the company, he was on a 747 bound for California.

"I was due to spend a month on test in America; until then, outside of trials events, I'd probably only ridden 500 miles on the road, so you really do have to question Norton's wisdom in choosing me. Prior to leaving I shared an office with Bob Manns, Norton's popular and experienced UK sales manager, who knew the trade and industry through and through; it was good training. If I'd had my way I would have gone to America and simply talked AJS, but selling road bikes was a dramatic change of culture."

The title of American sales manager in Long Beach, California, sounds glamorous, but as Mike discovered, the reality was very different.

"It was just an old aircraft production shed on a 3 acre site with an air-conditioned portacabin stuck on one end – certainly very different from an image of surf and swaying palm trees! Fortuitously just up the road in Paramount were the offices of *Motor Cycle Weekly*, a leading publication run by two English expats, Gavin Trippe and Bruce Cox."

The close proximity of *Motor Cycle Weekly* would later work to Norton's advantage, but the month's trial went well, and by August Mike was ensconced as NVC general manager USA, a position that, by arrangement, continued for the next two years. America of course is a large country, so I was intrigued to find out from Mike how big his 'sales patch' was, and how many staff he had.

"For the first year we only had seven states and shared the country with Berliner Corporation, based in New Jersey, but after twelve months we took over all of the states up to the Mississippi, which gave us twenty four. Incidentally, 70 per cent of the USA's population lives east of the Mississippi. Max Maxtead, who was a great character from the fifties racing scene, was our 'road man'. Max had spent much of his life working in England and knew 'everyone who was everyone'; after emigrating to America he'd been working for the Smiths Industries' importer Nysonger when he met Dennis Poore at the Long Beach show. Poore hired him on the spot."

With Max busy visiting dealers in his big blue V-8 Mercury car, this left Mike to promote the profile of both Norton and AJS. Like Greeves before them, they employed some clever publicity and PR; tactics which gave the bike-buying public an impression that they were a much bigger concern than they actually were! A full-page 'dolly bird' ad was inserted on a perpetuity basis in prestigious magazines like *Cycle* and *Cycle World*, and Norton continued to score highly in the all important (for Americans) acceleration tests. In the important 'Big 7' road test comparison feature in *Cycle* the Commando came out on top, beating all of its Japanese, European and American rivals in the process.

At that time the factory in England was making about 9000 bikes a year, 3000 of which were sold in the home and European market, 2500 by Berliner and 2500 by NVC out of Long Beach. Impressive sales figures from an outlet which totalled just nine personnel including Mike and Brian Slark.

By way of comparison, BSA/Triumph's West Coast setup employed 160 people, and even the vice-president's wife drove around in a company Cadillac.

The helmet-less Mike could be often seen cruising around on his 'company' Commando, for which in 1970 he recalled he could buy three (US) gallons of gas for less than a dollar! Sales of the AJS Stormer were also going well, and in '71/'72 nearly half of the total production run of 2000 bikes was sold stateside; the torquey 2-strokes proving an ideal tool for the popular hare & hounds desert races. These usually attracted 1000 competitors, including NVC's sales manager, who as the results show was still a useful rider.

"For the desert racing our Ajays were fitted with bigger tanks and more comfortable seats – they were very different to the multi-lap scrambles I'd experienced in England. A hare and hounds would consist of two fifty-mile loops, a hare scramble two loops of the same course, and a Grand Prix race (like Elsinore) ten laps of approximately ten miles. Usually they would be based around ghost towns and the riders were started off in groups with no corrected time."

Very different from his favoured English mud, but during the two years he was in California Mike had some impressive rides. 25th in his first Elsinore was followed by 8th and then 5th, while thanks to advice from Brian Slark his first Barstow to Vegas race netted a creditable 14th – this against a field of 3000!

"The race started off in two waves of 1600 riders, an hour apart, and 'Slarky' had cautioned how the distance between fuel stops was pretty lengthy, advising me to carry some extra fuel in a plastic container. As

On the AJS competing in the 1972 Mint 400 – a 400-mile desert race open to both cars and bikes. (Photo Mike Jackson archive)

Mike with the first Vee Max in the UK circa 1980 – in his hand a sparking plug lighter. (Photo Mike Jackson archive)

Off-Road Giants!

it transpired it was extremely good advice, because countless numbers of riders including myself spluttered to a halt, but fortunately I had enough 'top-up' to reach the next support crew, situated on one of the numerous dry lakes.

Hours after the first 2000 riders had reached the Vegas finish, out-of-time competitors were still arriving at the Caesar's Palace Hotel HQ. As Mike observed, it was a bizarre scene as dirty, open-piped motorcycles zoomed along the Strip, overtaking all the stretch-limos filled with theatregoers. For the racers, you see, the famous fountains proved an ideal place for cooling off and washing down the bikes!

It's now time to return to where we started, and I asked Mike about the *On Any Sunday* film premier and the outcome of his meeting with Steve McQueen.

"I'd been warned that Hollywood's finest surrounded themselves with shoals of profoundly shallow execs specifically for preventing any contact with outsiders, so buttonholing the man in this crowd might prove to be a tougher mission than anticipated. Noticing my unease, I was introduced to Steve by Joe Parkhurst, and we were soon exchanging anecdotes about Eric Cheney and so on. I asked McQueen his toughest two-wheel experience to date whereby, after thinking for a while, he said 'I guess when Bud Ekins was teaching me about changing tyres in less than five minutes. That was hard; it made my hands bleed.'

We had some more talk about why he'd raced in a local motocross at Indian Dunes under the pseudonym of Harvey Mushman, instead of that year's same-day Elsinore GP, as publicly announced. 'I needed the space,' he said. I then popped the $64,000 question by asking if he'd consider appearing on our 1973 Norton wall poster. His reply was positive, but he was contracted to all sorts of marketing people who were using his wrist for watches, torso for medallions and polo shirts and 'below the belt' for chinos and sneakers. He said he'd find out and would phone the following day, but warned me that it might be more than Norton would want to pay. True to his word he called with the figure the next day; sadly it would have wholly consumed our ad and promo budget for the next twelve months. Such was his agency's fee for endorsing our poster it would have put an additional (and unacceptable) £75 on the list price of every new Norton."

After two years in America, Mike was on the way home to a new position as Norton Villiers Europe sales director, but first it was decided he would 'take the long way' and visit some of Norton's importers in far flung places like Hawaii, New Zealand and Australia. However, what started out as a useful PR exercise ended up with Mike taking a detour to Japan for an emergency shopping trip.

"I was in Australia when I received a telephone call from Dennis Poore. Dennis stuttered down the phone that he urgently needed me to go to Japan to source some improved main bearings for the newly introduced Combat engine, which was suffering a plague of bottom-end failures."

Superior quality replacement bearings needed to be urgently sourced. By using the Norton importer Murayama (in Tokyo) as a base, Mike duly went 'shopping' for samples of Superblend bearings, and other components as well, on behalf of the purchasing dept back in Wolverhampton.

"This stock was too heavy and far too urgent to await my eventual return, so each day I'd box up the hardware and consign it to the UK by airfreight. When I finally got back home to England I brought a further heavy box as accompanied luggage. Despite arriving at midnight on the Saturday I had to take the materials to Dennis Poore's house in Ascot by 10.00am the next morning. Having been away from England since the previous Christmas, my wife was not overjoyed!"

Poore had already been warned by his design engineers that the Combat's cams were too 'fierce' for a production engine; his decision to go ahead proved to be unwise. The several thousand by now produced had triggered numerous warranty claims, and over 2000 bikes had to go back down the production line for reworking. It was an expensive mistake, but one for which he (Poore) assumed full responsibility. Some may have regarded Dennis Poore as rather cold, but he's remembered by Mike, "as a slave-driver, in the nicest possible way, but a super bloke for whom to work."

An off-the-cuff comment in Australia, however, earned Jackson the nickname of the 'Let Slip Manager', and it was a comment he thought might cause his dismissal.

"I was interviewed by an Australian journalist and let slip that we were bringing out an 850 next year; in no time Mick Woollett got hold of it, and it was front page news in the UK. It was certainly the biggest commercial clanger I'd committed, but Poore, when interviewed and ever the opportunist, said 'Oh yes, but alongside the existing 750 our new 850 will be much more expensive.'

You can imagine the possible repercussions, especially as we had a huge stockpile of 750s; I wasn't sacked, but received a hell of a lot of stick from my colleagues."

Despite the Combat fiasco Norton was still running at a profit, but on the horizon loomed the Meriden lock-in: an in-depth tale and worthy of a book in itself.

By the mid-seventies Mike had finally retired from competition – a career of more than twenty years which had included more than 1000 scrambles, trials and desert races and one in which – other than the incident with Ivor England – he'd remained remarkably free from injuries. However, I'll let Mike have the last word with his recollections from the 1958 Italian GP and an incident which saw him rushing for the first aid tent.

"In the first timed practice I was struggling at 15th fastest, and in the hard dusty conditions the arch-rival Mi-Val and Bianchi riders were filling the top six places on their exotic OHC 4-strokes. In their powder-blue overalls with diagonal stripes their mechanics were very distinctive, and in the second session I noticed they were unofficially timing all of the riders over a 100-yard section of the track. Presumably they considered it to be a crucial part of the lap, and halfway through, and for one lap only, I astounded them (and myself) by achieving 3rd fastest time. What happened you see was that a wasp had got lodged under my rugger jersey, and duly advised his presence in the only way he knew how. The resultant pain prompted the quickest bit of riding I've ever accomplished to the first aid tent, where the sting was smoothed by a young nurse who came from the same mould as Gina Lollabrigida. The perplexed mechanics later scrutinised the bike, but never did discover the reason for that extra burst of speed!"

Robin Rhind-Tutt leads the 700cc Royal Enfield of Tony Donadel/Alan Bird at Willoughby Hedge in August 1963.

The Wasp concern started out making specialist frames, becoming the world's premier maker of sidecar motocross outfits during the '70s. But there were plenty of other sides to the business.

CHAPTER 17
WASP – A STING IN THE TAIL

It's only too easy to reflect on the early 1970s as being dark days with the industry's major players tottering on the abyss, but thankfully it wasn't all doom and gloom, and there were some chinks of light. For many of our smaller off-road specialists order books were bulging, like down at New Milton where 95 per cent of the Rickman brothers' Metisse output was going to export. By 1974 it would win them the coveted Queens Award for Industry, but buoyant trade wasn't limited to the Rickmans. Eric Cheney's beautifully-crafted products were both equipping our ISDT teams and challenging the might of the motocross world, and in Wiltshire a proud Robin Rhind-Tutt was celebrating a whitewash at the European sidecar motocross championships.

Robin is a quiet and reserved man who has not sought publicity for himself, and it's quite possible you may not instantly recognize his name, but in off-road circles his company has earned an unparalleled worldwide reputation. The name of Wasp became a byword for British motocross success, and in a fifteen year period from the late sixties to the mid-eighties virtually monopolised the national, European and world sidecar scene.

The Wasp factory is situated on a small trading estate set in the beautiful Wyle valley village of South Newton near Salisbury, and it has been the company's headquarters for well over thirty years. At his home – which the company founder built largely himself – I was joined by former five times British sidecar enduro champion George Greenland. George has been a Wasp rider, development engineer and friend to Robin since the mid-sixties, and over coffee we relived those happy days when Wasp ruled the world.

Dotted around the walls of Robin and Maureen's home are numerous reminders of the company's past successes, including a poster from 1972 when not only did Robert Grogg take the European championship, but the next seven places were also filled by Wasp riders. This was prior to the days when charioteers were granted world championship status – this came in 1980, when perhaps somewhat predictably the inaugural crown was won by Wasp-mounted pair Bohler/Muller on their Yamaha XS 750 twin.

Although there are healthy reminders of the past the company is very much in the present, and the current upsurge of interest in classic motocross has created a steady turnover for both new equipment and spares. From the heady days of the late seventies when the workforce was 20-strong, it is now slimmed down to very much a family affair,

117

Off-Road Giants!

Nick Thompson in the lead at a very muddy TV scramble. (Photo Morton's archive)

with both Robin and his son, Paul, working on construction while Maureen looks after all the paperwork and spares orders.

They may have made their name in the sidecar field, but during the last eighteen years a substantial part of the company's output has been devoted to solos, and during our visit Paul was in the throws of completing a batch of Rickman Metisse motocross frames.

Constructed from bronze welded Reynolds 531 tubing which is then nickel plated, these all bear the hallmark of superb quality and craftsmanship for which the company is noted, and it's of a standard that the majority of manufacturers could only dream about.

Of course the Wasp name is synonymous with sidecars, and in the workshop a gleaming motocross outfit powered by one of their own 1000cc parallel twins had just been completed for proud new owner David Brookes. I started by asking Robin how Wasp started and also how his own motorcycling career had developed.

"There was no history of motorcycling in our family, but when I left school I landed an apprenticeship in the machine shop at the Boscombe Down experimental site and shortly afterwards bought myself a 350cc Velocette. Quite a number of the lads at work were keen motorcyclists and members of the local Kiwi club, so I started going along to a few meetings and after a while bought myself a Dot trials bike. I became a great fan of grass-track and met the future southern centre grass-track champion Mike Lane, who encouraged me to have a go myself. I was particularly interested in the way the bikes were engineered and the way they handled, especially the sidecars, whose constructors and riders always showed a lot of innovation and enterprise.

On the road I'd progressed to a BSA Gold Star, but following an accident in which the Goldie was damaged I decided to build my own grass outfit. This retained the BSA frame, but I discarded the teles and made up my own set of trailing link forks. This of course showed up the limitations with the frame and swinging arm, so during the course of the next winter I went about constructing my first complete machine."

What was patently clear was that much of the opposition's machinery looked both very home-brewed and tatty, so from the outset Robin put a lot of emphasis on aesthetics and quality of finish with the welding skills he had honed and perfected at Boscombe Down. On his own admission he was not a potential champion rider, but his mark one machine soon became noticed, and it wasn't long before people wanted replicas – including the future British motocross number one Mike Guilford.

At this stage the now famous Wasp name hadn't been invented, and as Robin explained this came about largely by chance.

"By the mid-sixties I'd started making some frames for motocross sidecars, and Mike Guilford was getting some good results in the British championships on his Triumph. In addition I'd made a few solo scramblers which were campaigned to good effect by Rob Jordan and Triss Sharp, and the first trials frame which I wrapped around another Triumph twin for George Greenland to ride. Mike was working for motorcycle dealer George Sawyer in Winchester at the time, and with 'his man' achieving considerable success he (George) offered to sell my bikes through his shop. I don't know to this day why George decided on the name, but he had some stickers made and we officially became Rhind-Tutt Wasp, although the first ones had the hyphen missing and we had to paint it in. More and more work was coming my way, but it was getting a bit out of hand as at this stage I was still holding down my day job in the machine shop at Boscombe Down. It was taking up virtually all my spare time, and often I would finish work at Boscombe and then be up most of the night making the bikes. In 1968 I decided to go full time, initially working on my own, but after a while I took on one of the village lads to help me with the welding, and a year later in 1969 Mike Guilford joined me. Sidecar motocross was getting very popular and soon demand was outstripping the production capability of my home workshop, so in 1971 we decided to move and bought the site at South Newton, where we've been ever since."

Not only did 1971 see Robin move to much bigger premises and take on extra staff, it also saw the inaugural European sidecar championships, with Wasp-mounted Dutchman Rikus Lubers lifting the crown. Soon almost anybody who was anybody in the sidecar motocross field was Wasp-mounted, with rasping Norton twins the usual choice of power plant – although later on Terry Good experimented to good effect with a shaft driven BMW. This was very much the same for the following decade, which saw the likes of Mike Guilford, Terry Good and the Millard brothers dominating the home championships and a plethora of continental riders including Lubers, Robert Grogg and German Reinhart Bohler scooping the European and later the world honours. Due in no small part to the way the engines were prepared by the trio of Tony Hall, George Greenland and Dave Lane the aging Norton twin was still competitive, but with the latter's demise and the 2-strokes starting to get on the pace a new engine was required. Robin takes up the story again.

Rob Jordan, unusually with both wheels of his Triumph Wasp on the ground in March 1966.

"SOON ALMOST ANYBODY
WHO WAS ANYBODY
IN THE SIDECAR
MOTOCROSS FIELD WAS
WASP-MOUNTED, WITH
RASPING NORTON TWINS
THE USUAL CHOICE OF
POWER PLANT"

Off-Road Giants!

Two times British champion Mike Guilford in action on his Triumph-engined Wasp. (Photo Morton's archive)

"I knew that the engine I wanted was a slightly forward canted 1000cc parallel twin, but nothing like that was available so I seriously considered making my own. But this was really dead in the water, as there was no way I could design and build an engine from scratch."

However, salvation to the problem was not far away in the form of specialist designers and engineers John Hardcastle and Alan Baker, who quickly warmed to Robin's engine concept.

"John wrote down what my requirements were and a few months later phoned to say that the first prototype was ready, so George Greenland and I drove up to the midlands to see it fire up. It was just how I envisaged it, but obviously at that time we had no idea how it might perform. After the initial run the engine was stripped and the major components meticulously examined by John and Alan for any wear. This took place two or three more times with the revs being gradually increased until they were happy for us to take it away for testing. We mated it up to a 4-speed gearbox which we'd had specially made, and fitted it into George's enduro outfit which he rode on the road, clocking up as many miles as he could testing the engine's durability. From the outset it was fantastic, producing a huge amount of torque, although with its high compression it wasn't too easy to start."

I can vouch that after having previously tried to start George's former championship winning machine this was a classic case of understatement, as I was hard pushed to kick it over, let alone start the beast. On the race track, however, this didn't prove to be a problem, with the Millard brothers soon on the top of the rostrum in the domestic championship and the impressive Reinhart Bohler clocking up wins in the world rounds. By now, with the improvement of water cooling, the lightweight 2-stroke hordes were closing in, and despite his best efforts Bohler was closely denied another world crown. In enduros where George Greenland continued to fly the Wasp flag he notched up

W Linz on his Bultaco-engined bike in the Scottish six days trial in the early seventies. (Photo Morton's archive)

Off-Road Giants!

Dick Ramplee and Sean Gray won the British sidecar enduro championship twice on this ex-George Greenland Norton Wasp outfit.

an impressive tally of five British championship titles, and was twice winner of the Le Touquet beach race on the booming twin. Such was George's dominance of the French sand race he was initially denied his second victory, because the lap scorers couldn't believe that he had completed five laps when his nearest rivals had only managed two. A German competitor had already been awarded the winner's trophy and departed for home, so much to the chagrin of the organisers they had to buy a second, which George later received broken in the post. His finish straight speed on the 1000cc twin was clocked at 114mph by an overhead helicopter pilot, and it gave Robin an insight into the engines potential in a road or tarmac racing application, which he told me about.

"In total we made about 50 engines, most of which were used for motocross or enduros, but we also made two 5-speeders that were housed in road-race frames and campaigned in the Battle of the Twins series. At the time BSA also showed an interest in it to power a road bike, so we made up a rolling test bed for it, and although it showed potential it would have required a lot of redesigning. This was especially with regard to eliminating the noise generated by the straight cut gears and overcoming impending new decibel limit legislation. It was always a difficult engine to start, especially on cold days, and I did go as far as machining a crankcase to incorporate an electric starter, although this wasn't pursued and the project was dropped.

George became very adept at starting the big twin, although prior to winter enduros he would often drain the oil overnight and warm it up on a camping stove before refilling it the next morning. We took one to a presentation party in Germany where someone bet George that he couldn't start it; I disappeared, although needless to say he got it fired up first kick! We did various experiments with the engine, including a one-up one-down firing sequence, but this created lubrication problems so we reverted to the tried and tested 180-degree crank."

Although much of the company's output was centred on motocross and enduro sidecars, the solos weren't forgotten, and over the years Robin has made well over 100 scrambles frames and fifty for trials. In the days before he became a sidecar enduro ace George Greenland was southern centre solo champion, and campaigned the 500cc Triumph-engined Wasp very successfully – well past what might have been regarded as its sell by date into the mid-1970s. A variety of other power units including Tiger cubs, C15s and B40s were fitted, although it wasn't all 4-strokes, and following a string of centre wins by Geoff Chandler, Bultacos became a popular choice of engine.

The 1000cc parallel twin was an expensive engine to produce, and the mid-eighties saw a downturn in the company's fortunes as on the race tracks the 2-strokes took centre stage. By his own admission Robin is not a great fan, and although they did make a few outfits powered by water-cooled 600cc 2-stroke singles, they gradually downsized motocross production and began to concentrate on the needs of the sidecar pilot on the road.

This was a niche sector of the motorcycle market but one which had an enthusiastic following, especially on the continent, where the riders demanded car-like handling and braking from their outfits. When fitted with leading link or hub-centred steered front ends, fat low profile car tyres and disc brakes, all married up to the performance potential of the present day motorcycle engine, the modern sidecar is a seriously impressive piece of machinery. Robin readily admits to loving a challenge, and soon not only was Wasp able to offer the complete package of leading links and fat tyres, but also experiment with its own version of hub steering. It began manufacturing a sports sidecar which was conceived and designed by Mike Guilford. Before we left, Robin showed me an example of one of these single seater chairs, which not surprisingly – given its family heritage – displayed all the famous Wasp hallmarks of neat detail touches and a superb quality of finish.

Today Robin is still busy, but now he manages to avoid working all night with his welding torch and gets time to devote to his own bike restoration projects and the ongoing extension work on his house. During his long career he may not have sought personal fame or recognition, but the bikes he created still reverberate around the motocross circuits of the world, and are a lasting legacy to his great vision, skill and enthusiasm for motorcycling. Robin Rhind-Tutt and Wasp: names that shaped the history of sidecar motocross.

INDEX

ACU 20, 70, 80, 108
AJS 16, 20, 46, 54, 58, 112
AMC 22, 24, 44, 50
Archer, Les 34, 50
Ariel 25, 33, 68

Banks, John 36, 47
Baraugh Bill 10, 28, 40, 62
BBC radio 102
Bickers, Dave 16, 18, 47
Big Bear 12, 29
Blakeway, Gordon 42
Brands Hatch 22
Brown, Fluff 54-59
Browning, Arthur 46
BSA 34, 40, 44, 74, 78, 88
Bultaco 12
Burton, John 'Burly' 72-76

Catalina GP 30

Cheney, Eric/Simon 10, 12, 32-37, 46, 76
Cheshire, Terry 10, 50, 62
Clayton, Dick 46
Coleman, Cliff 30
Comer, Dick 16
Comerfords 30, 72
Cotton 14, 15, 56
Cross Manufacturing, Bath 14, 15, 56
Curtis Dave 12, 42, 48-53
CZ 16, 44, 46, 47
Czech GP 60

Davis, Dickie 94
Davis, Ivor 12, 80, 86
Davis Malcolm 17, 46
De Coster, Roger 36, 44, 47
Denly, Monty 56
Dot 10, 40, 62
Draper, John 110

East Germany 13
Eastwood, Vic 11, 42, 44, 46
Ekins, Bud 12, 26-31, 64, 96
Ekins, Dave 30
England, Ivor 8, 87-92

Francis Barnett 10, 42, 62, 104, 110

Garmisch 10
Giant's Head 14, 91
Giles, Johnny 22, 28, 36, 77-86
Goss, Bryan 'Badger' 8, 14-19, 56
Grandstand trophy 14, 18, 34, 44, 76, 92
Great Escape, The 30
Greenland, George 117, 120, 122
Greeves 12, 16, 46, 62, 64, 106, 112
Greeves, Bert 16, 46, 65, 112
Grogg, Robert 117
Guilford, Mike 118, 122

123

Hallman, Torsten 16, 18
Hants GN 41, 43, 63, 76
Harvey, Roger 46
Hawthorn, Mike 38
Heanes, Ken 30, 31, 36, 56, 93-99
Hickman, Keith 36
Higher Farm Wick 16, 49, 62, 79
Hitchcock, Don 16
Hitchcock, Joe 24
Hooper, Rob 46
Horsell, Ian 12
Horsfield, Chris 38-47
Howdle, Peter 20
Hudson, Neil 19
Husqvarna 18

Inchley, Peter 58
International six days trial 12, 24, 30, 52, 62, 64, 80, 82, 93, 94
Isle of Man 13

Jackson, Gordon 20-25, 30, 78
Jackson, Mike 12, 106-116
James 39, 42
Jarrolim, Mr 46
Johnson Motors 28
Jones, Geraint 19
Jordan, Rob 119

Kawasaki 46
Kelly, Sean 31
Kendall, Ken 66-71
King, Max 100-105
KTM 19

Leadbitter, Tom 18

Maico 18
Martin, Brian 10, 44

Martin, Dean 28
Mann, Bob 28, 30, 96, 114
Matchems Park 10, 61, 88
Matchless 44
Mayes, Fred 18
MCC 104, 105
McCandless, Rex 32, 78
McQueen, Steve 12, 28, 30, 96, 116
Miller, Sammy 20, 25, 105
Montrieul 10
Moose Run 27
Moss, Stirling 38
Motocross des Nations 34, 50, 74
MZ 98

National service 10, 56, 62, 68, 80
Newman, Paul 28
Nichol, Dave 42
Nicholson, Billy 22, 30
Noyce, Graham 19
NVT 54, 112

Onions, Pat 56

Pease, John 36
Pinhard trophy 62
Plumstead 24, 28
Poore, Dennis 116
Pouncey, Jack 58
Preston Cobb, Derry 16, 62, 112, 114
Pullman, Arthur 70

Rickman brothers (Don & Derek) 8, 12, 18, 46, 50, 70, 87
Robert, Joel 18, 44
Roberton, Andy 46, 56, 58, 114

Sandiford, Jim 36
Scott, Jerry 8, 34, 38, 44

Scottish six days trial 20, 21, 84
Sharp, Bryan 8, 13, 60-65
Sharp, Pops 8, 12, 108
Sharp, Triss 8-13, 18
Sheene, Barry 58, 114
Smith, Don 100
Smith, Jeff 11, 16, 42, 44, 46, 50
Spanish GP 90
Starmaker 56, 57
Steen, John 30
Stillo, Ron 28
Stirland, Peter 13
Stonebridge, Brian 10, 12, 40, 50, 52

Taylor, Harold 17
Taylor, Rob 18
Tiblin, Ralph 38, 44
Timms, Jim 56, 57
Triumph 12, 26, 28, 77, 96
Trophee Des Nations 18
Turner, Edward 77

Usher, Ted 30

Venables, Ralph 23, 78, 82, 104
Victory trial 24
Viney, Hugh 22, 24, 50, 84, 104

Walker, Rob 90
Ward, Geoff 42, 50
Wasp 117-122
Welsh three day 96
West, Jock 28
West of England trial 83, 84, 100
Westlake, Rod 8
Wiggins, Graham 8
Wilkinson, Mick 36
Winsor, Gerald 18

Also from Veloce

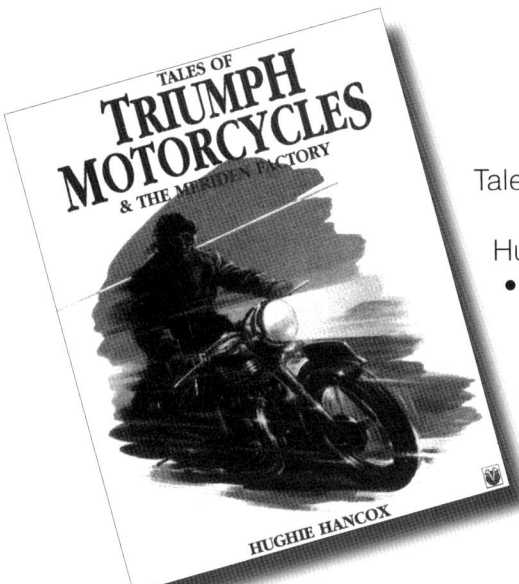

Tales of Triumph Motorcycles & the Meriden Factory

Hughie Hancox • Paperback • 25x20.7cm • £12.99*
• 144 pages • 91 b&w pictures • ISBN 978-1-901295-67-2

Hughie worked at Triumph from 1954 until its closure in 1974. Here's the story of his life in the famous Meriden factory; of many adventures with Triumph motorcycles & Triumph people. Records the fascinating history of a great marque.

Velocette Motorcycles – MSS to Thruxton

Rod Burris • Hardback • 25x20.7cm • £29.99* • 160 pages
• 308 colour & b&w photos • ISBN 978-1-904788-28-7

The definitive development history of the most famous Velocette motorcycles, based on the author's earlier work, out of print for many years and much sought-after today. Includes the most comprehensive appendices ever published on this historic marque.

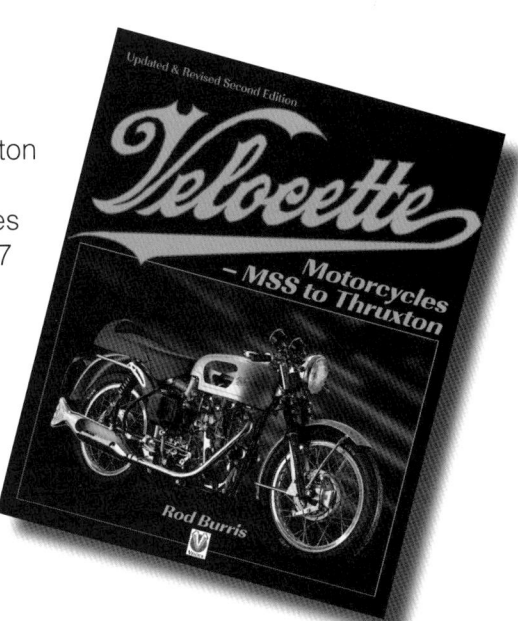

British 250cc Racing Motorcycles 1946-1959

Chris Pereira • Hardback • 25x20.7cm • £15.99* • 80 pages
• 97 monochrome photographs • ISBN 978-1-904788-12-6

The history and development of the privately-built, British 250cc specials and hybrids raced in Britain from 1946 to 1959, recalling the men and machines involved in what was clearly the most innovative class of road racing in the 1950s.

*All prices subject to change, p&p extra • www.veloce.co.uk
• info@veloce.co.uk • Tel. +44 (0) 1305 260068

MOTORCYCLE APPRENTICE – MATCHLESS IN NAME AND REPUTATION

Bill Cakebread

A young Londoner had only one ambition in life – to work with motorcycles. That simple wish led to an apprenticeship that was to change Bill Cakebread's life forever, as the training that Associated Motorcycles Limited provided enabled achievements he never dreamed possible. This book gives a unique insight to the atmosphere and excitement of working in a motorcycle factory. It is an inspiring story, supported by a host of period photographs and rare documents, which provides a fascinating record of work within the British motorcycle industry in the final years of its decline into oblivion.

£19.99 • Hardback • 100 colour and b&w pictures • ISBN 978-1-84584-179-9

To order any Veloce titles, visit us on the web at www.veloce.co.uk / www.velocebooks.com

EDWARD TURNER – THE MAN BEHIND THE MOTORCYCLES

Jeff Clew

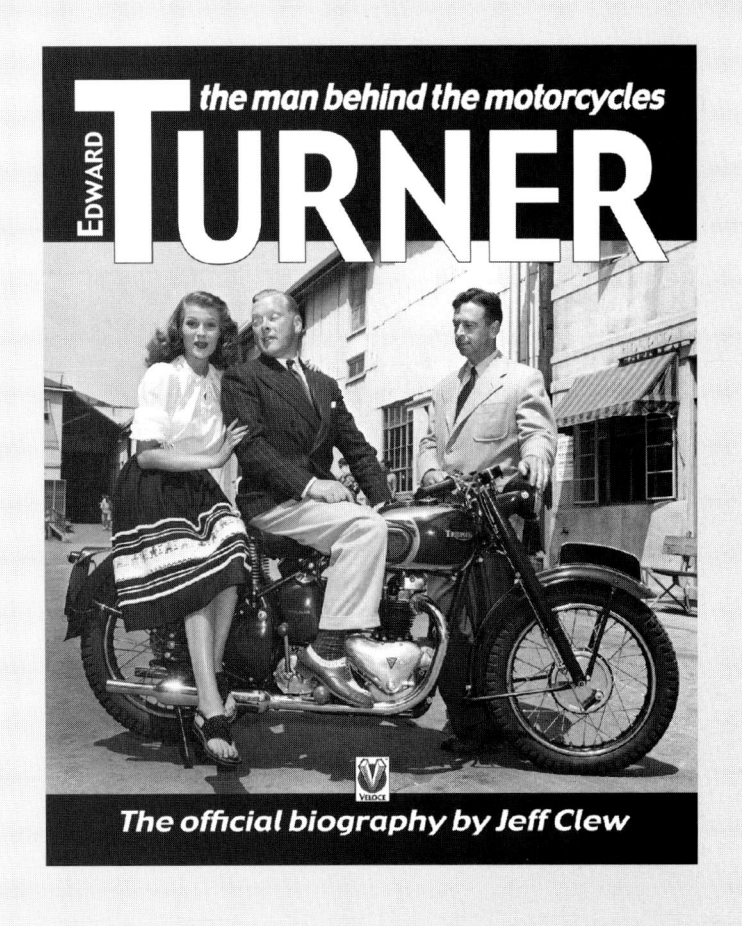

For the first time the life of Edward Turner, one of Britain's most talented motorcycle designers, is revealed in full. Although seen by many as an irascible man who ran a very tight ship, it is an inescapable fact that his was a highly profitable company. His hugely successful sales campaign after World War 2 stunned America's own manufacturers and had long-lasting repercussions on their own home market. Turner was an inventive genius with a flair for pleasing shapes and an uncanny ability to perceive what the buying public would readily accept, and then produce it at the right price. This is his story.

£17.99 • Paperback • Over 100 colour and b&w pictures • ISBN 978-1-845840-65-5

email info@veloce.co.uk, or telephone us on 01305 260068. Prices subject to change, p&p extra.

THE TRIUMPH TIGER CUB BIBLE

Mike Estall

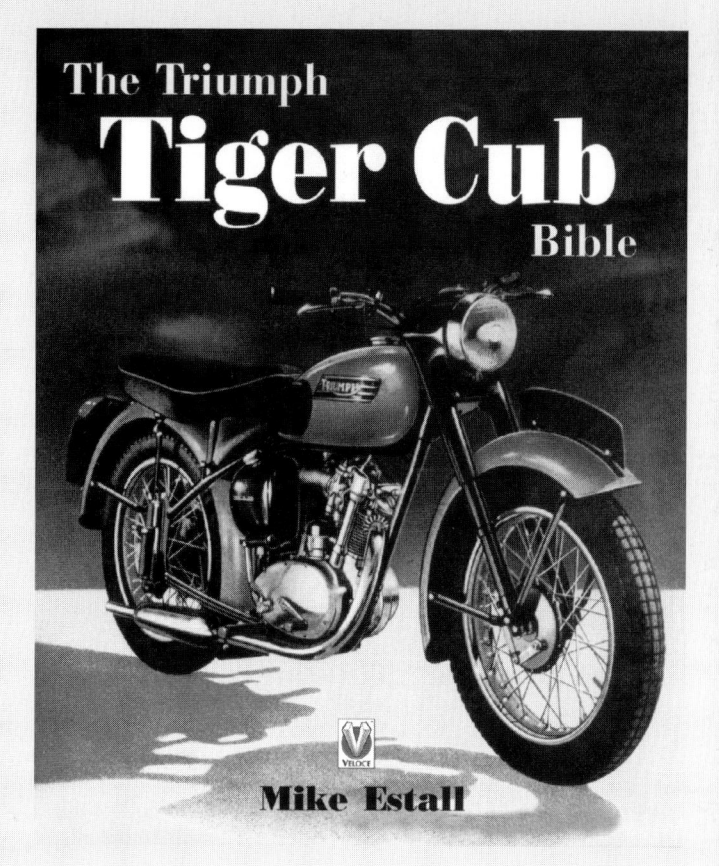

The full international history of the popular Triumph Tiger Cub and Triumph Terrier motorcycles. This ultimate reference source covers every aspect of these machines, including 22 detailed model profiles, delivery details of 113,000 individual machines to 153 countries, and technical design specifications of engine and transmission components, lubrication, fuel and electrical systems. Military, police and competition bikes are covered, plus the full story behind the model's production run.

£35 • Hardback • Over 200 b&w pictures • ISBN 978-1-904788-09-6

www.veloce.co.uk / www.velocebooks.com